Other Titles of Interest

ARNOLD, G.
Economic Co-operation in the Commonwealth

BUNTING, G. R. & LEE, M. J.
Evolution of the United Nations

BURLEY, J. & TREGEAR, P.
African Development and Europe

EVANS, G.
War on Want

HUGHES, D. J.
Science and Starvation

MAZRUI, A. A.
The Anglo-African Commonwealth

OSBORNE, M.
Region of Revolt: Focus on Southeast Asia

PERGAMON INTERNATIONAL L
of Science, Technology, Engineering an
The 1000-volume original paperback library
industrial training and the enjoymen
Publisher: Robert Maxwell,

THE COMMONWI
A NEW LOC

THE PERGAMO
INSPECTION CC

An inspection copy of any book published in
be sent to academic staff without obligation
recommendation. Copies may be retained fo
if not suitable. When a particular title is ado
and the recommendation results in a sale of
retained with our compliments. The Publi
revised editions and new titles to be publi

THE COMMONWEALTH:
A NEW LOOK

BY

ANDREW WALKER

Author of *The Modern Commonwealth*

PERGAMON PRESS

OXFORD · NEW YORK · TORONTO · SYDNEY
PARIS · FRANKFURT

U.K.	Pergamon Press Ltd., Headington Hill Hall, Oxford OX3 0BW, England
U.S.A.	Pergamon Press Inc., Maxwell House, Fairview Park, Elmsford, New York 10523, U.S.A.
CANADA	Pergamon of Canada Ltd., 75 The East Mall, Toronto, Ontario, Canada
AUSTRALIA	Pergamon Press (Aust.) Pty. Ltd., 19a Boundary Street, Rushcutters Bay, N.S.W. 2011, Australia
FRANCE	Pergamon Press SARL, 24 rue des Ecoles, 75240 Paris, Cedex 05, France
FEDERAL REPUBLIC OF GERMANY	Pergamon Press GmbH, 6242 Kronberg-Taunus, Pferdstrasse 1, Federal Republic of Germany

First edition 1978

British Library Cataloguing in Publication Data

Walker, Andrew, b. 1926
The Commonwealth: A New Look
1. Commonwealth of Nations
I. Title
909'.09'712410827   DA18   77-20254

ISBN 0-08-021823 7 Hardcover
       0-08-021824 5 Flexicover
       0-08-023014 8 Flexicover non-net

Printed in Great Britain by Netherwood Dalton & Co. Ltd., Huddersfield

Contents

Foreword

One of the great problems of the contemporary Commonwealth is to spread understanding of what it is and what it does. Our transformation has been so rapid, our evolution into new forms of international co-operation so complete, that many people perhaps understandably find that the reality of today is concealed by the myths of the past.

Andrew Walker's study of Commonwealth activity is all the more welcome in that it comes from a commentator independent of Governments and of pressure groups. It describes the vast range of Commonwealth co-operation, which exists only because the participants find it useful to work together, and it indicates that this day-to-day practical endeavour is both grounded upon and itself nourishes a vast fund of goodwill across the lines of demarcation — and sometimes of confrontation — that too often seem to threaten the world with disharmony. I welcome the publication of this most useful book.

SHRIDATH RAMPHAL
Commonwealth Secretary-General

Introduction

One of the minor ironies of life is that practical co-operation between Commonwealth countries has increased enormously at a time when many people regard the institution as virtually moribund. Some of this co-operation has been deliberately fostered by governments, who see in the Commonwealth a useful instrument for certain aspects of economic and social development; some is the work of individuals serving a cause. Most of it is quiet and unspectacular, virtually unreported and therefore unknown.

This book is an attempt to remedy the deficiency by describing in outline the vast amount of co-operative endeavours carried out under the Commonwealth umbrella. It is not the first attempt, and I gladly pay tribute to Derek Ingram, whose book *The Commonwealth at Work* (also published by Pergamon Press) pioneered this field. But his book dates from 1969, and there have been great changes in the scene since then. Many projects, such as the youth programme and the fund for technical co-operation, didn't even exist in 1969. Others — the Commonwealth Secretariat and the Commonwealth Foundation, for example — were still fairly new and have developed enormously in the intervening years.

This book, then, contains a great deal of information which has never appeared in this form before. Its title has a double meaning, since the Commonwealth itself has acquired a new look in the past decade. I hope it will provide useful source material for those interested not only in the Commonwealth as such but also in Third World studies and international relations generally. It may also interest people in the various professions in which Commonwealth links have been forged — which means virtually all of them, with particular emphasis on education, law and medicine.

It is not, though, the work of an academic but of a journalist, one who has been covering Commonwealth affairs in print and on the air for a number of years and has visited many of the member countries. Although it is largely factual, personal opinions do creep in. They are those of a middle-aged, middle-class Briton, although perhaps not typical of that particular sub-species. There is plenty of room for argument over the directions the Commonwealth is taking, and in the last chapter, which tries to peer a little ahead, I have constructed a sort of patchwork quilt of ideas, my own and those of others. The aim is not to argue a case — it's all far too sketchy for that — but to suggest a few lines of thought.

A book of this nature could not have been written without a great deal of help. Many members of the staff of the Commonwealth Secretariat, the Commonwealth Parliamentary Association, the Commonwealth Institute and other bodies gave up their time to explain to me what they were trying to achieve. I gratefully acknowledge their help and at the same time absolve them of all responsibility for the result.

CHAPTER ONE

What Is The Commonwealth?

The Commonwealth? It doesn't exist any more does it?

We turned our backs on the Commonwealth when we entered the EEC.

The Commonwealth? It's a conglomeration of hostile nations, hostile to Britain.

These are among the comments made by people interviewed at random in London early in 1976. Allowing for a slight variation in the viewpoint, they could equally well have been made in any other Commonwealth capital — Lagos, for example, or Delhi or Canberra.

Now here are some comments of a very different type:

The Commonwealth . . . has provided the means by which countries have learned to consult and co-operate, despite differences in political systems, stages of economic development and racial origin.

The Commonwealth is our window on the world. Over the years its importance will deepen.

The Commonwealth is perhaps the most widely misunderstood association there could be.

These are among remarks made at different times in the past few years by statesmen who have worked closely together in a Commonwealth context and so are familiar with how the association has developed. Clearly there is a wide gap between the way they see it and the popular conception, a gap which gives particular point to the last quotation. It is certainly widely misunderstood.

Of course, this could apply to most international institutions. If you were to buttonhole the first dozen people you met in the street and ask them what they knew about the United Nations or the European-Community, you would get some curious answers, like the man who

1

thought the EEC was something to do with television licences.

But — it can be argued — the Commonwealth should surely be different. After all, it is a vital part of the history of all the member countries. Many people have the personal experience of being among the governed or the governing. As a British Prime Minister once remarked, nearly everybody in Britain has at least one relative living in another part of the Commonwealth. There are ties of kinship and common interest, so people in Commonwealth countries should know more about each other and understand each other better than do people in other countries. Or should they?

Perhaps it's this very appeal to history and kinship which prevents a proper understanding of what the Commonwealth is all about today — at least, as seen by those closely concerned in its activities. Looking back, we can see that the association evolved from the British Empire. Everybody knows that, even if the details aren't always clear. But what it has become bears no more resemblance to the British Empire than a butterfly does to a chrysalis. In the words of the present Secretary-General of the Commonwealth, it is the very negation of Empire.

This is difficult to grasp. For most people — and not only the British — Commonwealth relations mean relations between Britain and one of the other members. This view is obsolete. Despite its origins, the Commonwealth of today is not British. Britain is one member, still the most powerful but only one among thirty-six. It is not even an association of like-minded people; what, after all, do a Canadian, a Zambian and an Indian have in common? The people of the Commonwealth are as diverse as it is possible to be. It is not a federation or a military or economic bloc. The political systems of its members range from "the libertarian through the authoritarian to the incredible". It has no constitution, no rules, it conforms to no pattern known previously.

There are so many things that the Commonwealth is not that it is difficult to explain what it is except by analogy[1] or words which tend to be mystical, woolly and misleading. The simple but uninspiring description is that it is a voluntary association of countries whose

(1) Two favourite analogies are those of a family and a bridge (between peoples). Neither is exact. No family contains so many dissimilar members as the Commonwealth. A bridge stretches between two single points only; the Commonwealth is multilateral.

histories were intertwined for a period and therefore have certain things in common, such as language and working methods. They find it an advantage to remain loosely associated, because it helps them to co-operate in a number of ways which are of benefit to their people. This may not sound much, but for many people working in the Commonwealth it contains the promise of something much more precious — an example of co-operation across racial, geographical and economic barriers which can help bring together a divided world.

This book describes the co-operation which exists at present, with a hint of the directions it may take in the future. But it's as well to start at the beginning and explain how this curious institution came about. Although looking back at the Commonwealth purely as something in the past is misleading it's still as well to understand the way it evolved. The chrysalis, after all, is a necessary stage in the creation of the butterfly. (Those familiar with the historical outline can skip the rest of this chapter.)

There are various generalisations which can be made about how the Commonwealth came about. It can be argued that the British had lofty ideals about self-government and that their subject peoples forced them to put these ideals into practice. Or that when the British met opposition they at first tried bullying tactics and, if these failed, resorted to conciliation. Or that decisions taken to deal with one situation became precedents for action in another. All these explanations contain an element of truth. But the essential point is that the Commonwealth of today is a joint creation, produced by the interaction of a number of different peoples.

What they have created is unique. In the words of the Duke of Edinburgh, nothing quite like it has ever happened before. Empires have risen in the past, and, when they have come to an end, they have faded away like old soldiers. The British Empire evolved into something new, an experiment in international relations which is still in the process of development.

Part of the explanation lies in the way it grew as an empire. There is a well-known quotation by the 19th century historian, Sir John Seeley: "We seem to have conquered and peopled half the world in a fit of absence of mind. " There was some poetic licence in this — it was never more than a quarter of the world, and the traders and slave owners and founders of settlements weren't all that absent-minded; they knew what the word profit meant. But the point he was making was essentially true. The British Empire wasn't planned by politicians or civil servants. It came about over the course of several centuries through isolated acts of military conquest, trade and settlement by individuals, although, of course, the crown granted the charters which made the last two possible. Trade could be carried on anywhere in the world, but for Europeans settlement could be undertaken only where the climate was suitable and the native inhabitants weren't strong enough to resist successfully. As far as Britain was concerned that meant North America, Australia, New Zealand and southern Africa.

There was an important distinction between these colonies of settlement, where millions of people from the British Isles went to live permanently, and territories like India or parts of Africa, where a handful of officials governed huge areas but mostly went home to Britain when they retired. Colonies of the latter sort were sometimes acquired from other European powers as the result of peace treaties and sometimes by outright military conquest. India, the jewel in the imperial crown, became British because a trading company — the East India Company — filled the vacuum left by the collapse of the Mogul Empire.

In all this there was a strong economic motive. The original British — and European — expansion into the rest of the world was largely economic in origin, and until the nineteenth century British colonies were regarded as assets to be used purely for the benefit of the mother country. Their trade was strictly regulated. On the other hand the inhabitants of the colonies of settlement were affected by the ideas of democracy and freedom as these came to make themselves felt in Britain and this inevitably led to conflict.

The first colonies of settlement were in North America, and it was there that the Commonwealth may be said to have been born, There was a large French colony in what we now know as Canada — about 100 000, mostly in Quebec province. In 1759 General Wolfe captured Quebec — dying in the process — and the British found they had to administer this large group of foreigners. Most of the British in North America were rabid Protestants, but the French were allowed to retain their own language and the Roman Catholic religion.

During the American War of Independence which followed a few years later — and was, one might say, the first example of decolonisation, although an involuntary one — the French Canadians stayed loyal to the crown. They were joined by a large number of English-speaking loyalists from further south, who had no wish to be part of the United States. Two Canadian provinces were formed, Upper Canada (now Ontario), mostly English-speaking, and Lower Canada (now Quebec), mostly French-speaking.

However, during the nineteenth century the old form of colonial government became increasingly unpopular, in every sense of the word. There was an elected assembly in each province, it was true, but the real power was in the hands of the governor appointed from London, and there was conflict between the two. In the 1830s there were armed uprisings in each of the Canadian provinces, and, although they were not very serious, the British government was sufficiently alarmed to send a commissioner to Canada to investigate the grievances of the colonists. The man it chose was the first Earl of Durham.

Lord Durham diagnosed the problems inherent in the existing system and by the changes he recommended secured himself a position as founder of the Commonwealth from which later, cooler assessments were not able to displace him. In the words of Professor Nicholas Mansergh:

"For more than a century at least no discussion of imperial or Commonwealth constitutions, whether for Australia, or South Africa, for India or Ceylon, for Nigeria, Kenya or the West Indies, was complete without a first reference to the seminal contribution of that moody nobleman, with his dramatic good looks and volatile, uncomfortable temperament . . . with his radical opinions, his aristocratic connections and his great wealth . . . who by a brief visit of inquiry to British North America had impressed his personality upon the politics of imperial reform as surely as his father-in-law, Earl Grey, by presiding over the passage of the first Reform Bill, had enrolled his name on the page of English domestic history."[2]

The "moody nobleman" saw that the fundamental error was the entire separation of legislative and executive powers — the natural

(2) *The Commonwealth Experience* by Nicholas Mansergh (1969).

error of governments desiring to be free of the check of representative institutions, as he put it. "It may fairly be said" (he wrote) "that the natural state of government in these colonies is that of collision between the executive and the representative body. In all of them the administration of public affairs is habitually confided to those who do not co-operate harmoniously with the popular branch of the legislature; and the government is constantly proposing measures which the majority of the Assembly reject and refusing its assent to bills which that body has passed."

The solution he proposed was that of responsible government, which later became taken for granted in the Commonwealth. What it meant was that the colonial governor, while still owing allegiance to the crown, should entrust the administration to those who could command majority support in the Assembly, instead of to his appointed officials — in other words, cabinet government of the kind that had been introduced in Britain itself. In addition, the colonial administration should have freedom to legislate in domestic affairs, with the government in London having responsibility only for matters of imperial concern, such as changes in the constitution and relations with other countries.

Lord Durham also advocated a union of the two Canadian provinces, so that the French-speaking inhabitants of Lower Canada could be absorbed in a predominantly British territory. "I expected to find a contest between a government and a people; I found two nations warring in the bosom of a single state; I found a struggle not of principles but of races; and I perceived that it would be idle to attempt any amelioration of laws or institutions until we could first succeed in terminating the deadly animosity that now separates the inhabitants of Lower Canada into the hostile divisions of French and English."

The union was carried out almost immediately. Responsible government had to wait a few more years, and then it was granted first not to the province of Canada but to Nova Scotia. The Colonial Secretary, Lord Grey, sent the following message to the governor: "It cannot be too distinctly acknowledged that it is neither possible nor desirable to carry on the government of any of the British provinces in North America in opposition to the opinion of the inhabitants."

This principle was to be applied in time to all the colonies of settlement. The other North American provinces received reponsible government over the next few years, and in 1867 they joined in a federation, the Dominion of Canada. The settlements in Australia, New Zealand and South Africa were also granted responsible government. After the Boer War at the turn of the century the British South African provinces were joined with those of the Afrikaaners — who were ultimately of Dutch descent — to form the Union of South Africa.

This group of countries, together with Britain, formed the original Commonwealth. It was a predominantly British club, although in Canada there was a large French-speaking minority and in South Africa a black majority, as well as a large and intermittently hostile group of Afrikaaners. The idea of calling it a Commonwealth seems to have originated with Lord Rosebery, at one time British Foreign Secretary, who addressed an Australian audience in Adelaide with these words: "Does the fact of being a nation imply separation from the Empire? God forbid! There is no need for any nation, however great, leaving the Empire, because the Empire is a commonwealth of nations."

This was in 1884, but it was not until the early twentieth century that the word came into common use to describe Britain and her self-governing colonies. A commonwealth is a political community, and when the various Australian states came together as a federation in 1901 they called it the Commonwealth of Australia. There was no reason why this commonwealth should not exist within the larger one, and the word came to be used in a variety of ways — the British Commonwealth, the Commonwealth of Nations, the Imperial Commonwealth, for example. In 1917 during the first world war General Smuts of South Africa coined the phrase British Commonwealth of Nations which he applied to "the so-called dominions, a number of nations and states, almost sovereign, almost independent, who govern themselves." He added: "The man who would discover the real appropriate name for this vast system of entities would be doing a great service not only to this country (Britain) but to constitutional theory."

However, at the time he spoke it was not so much a name that was needed as a more precise explanation of the extent of self-government enjoyed by these almost sovereign nations. An imperial federation had been suggested but had been decisively turned down by the dominion governments themselves under the impact of growing nationalism. The first war accelerated the growth of that nationalism. The problem was that, although the dominions willingly contributed men and materials for the prosecution of the war, they had no say in its direction at the highest level and were consulted hardly at all by the British government.

The idea of an imperial war cabinet, including ministers from the dominions, was tried in 1917 and again in 1918, but, while it proved popular in the exceptional conditions of a common struggle, it did not survive the war. Instead the dominions sought and were eventually granted complete independence.

The formula arrived at as an acknowledgement of this independence was in the Balfour report, which was adopted at the imperial conference of 1926. This defined the status of Britain and her dominions as follows: "They are autonomous communities within the British Empire, equal in status, in no way subordinate one to another in any aspect of their domestic or external affairs, though united by a common allegiance to the Crown, and freely associated as members of the British Commonwealth of Nations." This sonorous declaration, with its echoes of the Athanasian Creed, was formalised in the Statute of Westminster, passed by the British Parliament in 1931.

It is the basis on which the modern Commonwealth rests, although the common allegiance to the Crown is in the case of a majority of the members entirely symbolic. They are republics and recognise the Queen as Head of the Commonwealth but not as their own head of state. It applied, of course, only to the white dominions until after the second world war.

The great problem in 1945, when the war was over, was what to do about India. Indian nationalists had campaigned tirelessly for independence since the 1920s. Gandhi taught them to fight by non-violent means, but they didn't learn the lesson very well, and there was considerable bloodshed on the road to independence. The Muslims mistrusted the Hindus and demanded their own separate state of Pakistan. There was a Labour government in Britain, and it was perfectly willing — in fact, eager to give India its independence. Faced with this conflict it finally agreed with reluctance to partition India, so that it became two countries instead of one. India and Pakistan became independent in 1947 and applied for membership of the Common-wealth.

Because this is the way it happened we are inclined to take it for granted. But it was by no means inevitable. Indian nationalists had been uncertain that dominion status would give them the full indepen-dence they sought. Paradoxically it was the example of two nations being allowed to secede — the Irish Republic and Burma — which apparently enabled them to accept that Commonwealth membership was compatible with national freedom. In the case of India another reason was that Pakistan intended to join in any case and, left to itself, might give the association an anti-Indian stance.

India's first prime minister, Mr. Nehru, put it rather differently: "We join the Commonwealth obviously because we think it is benefi-cial to us and to certain causes in the world that we wish to advance. The other countries of the Commonwealth want us to remain because they think it is beneficial to them . . . In the world today, where there are so many disruptive forces at work, where we are often at the verge of war, I think it is not a safe thing to encourage the breaking-up of any association one has . . . it is better to keep a co-operative association going which may do good in this world rather than break it." It is not a bad argument in favour of the Commonwealth, even though it hardly betrays any marked enthusiasm.

The decision of India, Pakistan and, a little later, Ceylon, to join the Commonwealth was a vital stage in the development of the associa-tion. The Commonwealth of today would not exist if a different deci-sion had been made. It has been argued that an all-white Common-wealth would have corresponded more closely to the reality of "kith and kin", but it is doubtful whether such an association would have survived. In any case the question did not arise. Instead of a white man's club, the Commonwealth became a meeting-point of different races. Inevitably it became less intimate. It lost the close collaboration which had marked the war years, but it gained in a widening of its horizons.

Indian membership depended on the acceptance by the other members of its republican status. After some heart-searching this status was accepted. It is to the credit of the other nations that it was. They decided in the end that it was more important to have India as a member than to hold fast to what until then had been seen as the only constitutional link between the members. Since those days, of course, republicanism has become the fashion among the developing nations in the Commonwealth, and the monarchies are a minority. The reason is straightforward enough. Leaders of many countries which are newly independent don't feel that their independence is complete as long as a queen from elsewhere is their head of state.

The fact that Asian countries could become members of the Commonwealth meant that the way was now open for people of all races. However, in practice it took a number of years before the peoples of Africa, the Pacific and the Caribbean were freed. In the 1950s and even in the first year or two of the 60s it was still possible to speak of the British Empire. The forces of nationalism in Africa and elsewhere were gathering momentum but they had not yet carried everything before them. In parts of Africa — notably Kenya and Rhodesia — there were sizeable numbers of white people, and the British government's original intention was to create multi-racial partnerships in those countries.

To the Africans, who saw that in spite of their vastly greater numbers they were to be the junior partners, this was an unwelcome idea, and their leaders campaigned against it. In 1960 the British Prime Minister, Mr. Harold Macmillan, toured the African continent and spoke to many of these leaders. At the end of his tour he told the South African Parliament in Cape Town: "The wind of change is blowing through the continent."

The South Africans were not unduly impressed, and the following year they left the Commonwealth because the other members criticised their racial policies. But for Britain, Mr. Macmillan's speech was the signal for an unprecedented act of decolonisation — or more accurately a series of acts. Colonies would be given independence at the rate of two or three a year — too soon and too quickly, many people grumbled.

The reasons for this hasty dismantling of the British Empire are varied. Among them is the fact that Britain was no longer a great power and, tired by her efforts in the war, couldn't face the prospect of holding subject races down by force. In the words of one statesman of the time, the British had lost their will to rule. This is doubtless an important part of the explanation, but there were other factors. The end of empire coincided with the first attempt to join the other countries of Europe in the EEC. It was a change of direction, from being a country which looked over the distant seas to one which concentrated on its own backyard — a change which many found distressing. And we should not, I think, forget the strain of idealism which used to run through British life, as, for example, in the campaign to end slavery and in this century the movements supporting colonial freedom. Idealism has now practically vanished from the mainstream of British politics, which are increasingly the preserve of the loud-mouthed and the slick. Yet many Commonwealth leaders today can testify to the enormous influence British political idealists of yesterday have had on their thinking and their attitudes to Britain itself.

With the granting of independence to the colonies of Africa, the Caribbean, the Pacific and the Mediterranean, the Commonwealth of today took its final shape. The leaders of most of the newly independent countries came to the same conclusion as Mr. Nehru — that it was better to keep a co-operative association going than to break it. Membership therefore rose, and by 1976 had reached thirty-six.

Not all are nations of the first rank. Seychelles, for instance, has about sixty-thousand people. Nauru has only about six thousand. Nevertheless, just as all men are equal in the sight of God, so all members are of equal standing in the Commonwealth. Their diversity within a loose framework of unity gives the association its special "flavour" and has enabled it to carve out its own role in economic and social development. The following chapters of this book are an attempt to describe this role.

CHAPTER TWO

"A Candour Unknown Elsewhere"

Commonwealth leaders have been in the habit of consulting each other about the issues of the day for nearly a hundred years, although the form and content of their discussions have changed considerably.

When Queen Victoria celebrated her golden jubilee in 1887 her Prime Minister, Lord Salisbury, summoned a colonial conference "for the discussion of those problems which appear more particularly to demand attention at the present time". The attendance was by present standards a little eccentric — a handful of premiers of self-governing colonies and a number of private individuals with an interest in imperial affairs.

Lord Salisbury remarked with some prescience: "The decisions of this conference may not be, for the moment, of vital importance; the business may seem prosaic and may not issue in any great results at the moment. But we are all sensible that this meeting is the beginning of a state of things which is to have great results in the future."

The business was certainly prosaic. About half the time of the conference, which lasted twenty days, was taken up with discussions on defence. The British government, concerned at increasing naval competion from continental countries, wanted the colonies to make some contribution to imperial defence; this was an argument which continued on and off until the first world war. Other subjects included postal and telegraphic communications and the question of a trans-Pacific cable, a report on the Canadian Pacific Railway and various other technical matters.

Lord Salisbury made it clear that schemes of imperial federation, which had already been mooted by some enthusiasts, were certainly not a matter for discussion, except perhaps at some undefined time in the future. This, too, was an argument which was to be carried on for many years. Indeed, at the next colonial conference ten years later (during Queen Victoria's diamond jubilee) the idea of a closer link between the countries of the Empire received encouragement.

The chairman was the Colonial Secretary, Joseph Chamberlain, one of the few figures in British political life to have been a whole-hearted imperialist. He made the personal suggestion of what he called "a great council of the Empire" to which the colonies would send representatives. It might, he said, slowly grow to that federal council "to which we must always look forward as our ultimate ideal".

However, the representatives of the colonies did not look forward to a federal council as their ultimate ideal, and Chamberlain's suggestion was not proceeded with. The federal idea cropped up in various forms at conferences during the early part of the twentieth century but never met with general acceptance. It found some favour with New Zealand for a time — New Zealand having always been the most British of the colonies and the furthest away — but both South Africa and Canada were suspicious of any proposals which would have the effect of limiting their freedom of action.

The conference of 1897 set the pattern for imperial and, later, Commonwealth conferences. It was attended only by the premiers of the self-governing colonies, and its proceedings were in private, two conventions which have lasted to this day.

In the early years of the twentieth century the conferences were put on a more regular footing than previously. In 1907, when the self-governing colonies were re-named dominions, it was decided that they should be known as imperial conferences and held every four years to discuss matters of common interest. From the Australian government came the idea of a conference secretariat to replace the "impenetrability and remoteness" of the Colonial Office which at that time organised the conferences. The British Colonial Secretary, Lord Elgin, expressed opposition to it on the grounds that it might impair the responsibility which all the member governments owed to their own parliaments. It was to be many years before the idea of a secretariat was accepted, and even then British acceptance was reluctant.

After the first world war the imperial conferences were dominated by the desire of the dominions to define their status. In practice, as the war had demonstrated, they were the equals of Britain, but legally they were still subordinate to the British Parliament. Canada and South Africa were again in the van of the movement for complete independence. Nor was the fight without some bitterness. It is not only the modern Commonwealth which goes in for controversy.

Here, for instance, is a diary entry made by the Canadian Prime Minister, Mr. Mackenzie King, at the time of the 1923 conference: "Lord Derby rather tried to force my hand in the matter of how far the dominions might be expected to go with respect to the Empire being attacked at any point. I felt obliged to interrupt him and to point out that Canada's co-operation could not be taken for granted. It was an unpleasant and somewhat trying experience. However, it constitutes to my mind the most important of all the statements made at the present conference." For his part, the British Foreign Secretary, Lord Curzon found Mackenzie King "obstinate, tiresome and stupid".

In the end obstinacy and tiresomeness — if not stupidity — paid off, and, as we have seen, the dominions had their complete independence recognised in legal form by the Statute of Westminster.

By that time (1931) there were new preoccupations in the form of the world economic slump. In 1932 there was an imperial economic conference in Ottawa, from which came the system of imperial (later, Commonwealth) preference which lasted almost to the present day. In the catastrophe of the economic crisis Britain had abandoned her policy of free trade, and by giving preferences to primary products from Commonwealth countries and receiving them for manufactured goods she seemed to some people to be laying the foundations for a new economic system. The supporters of free trade within the Empire were enthusiastic and vocal in the 1930s, with Lord Beaverbrook's *Daily Express* as their mouthpiece. The idea was briefly revived in the sixties as an alternative to British membership of the EEC. But by that time it was clear that the Commonwealth could never be an economic bloc.

The last imperial conference was in 1937. The war intervened, and the meetings were not resumed until 1944, when they were renamed Commonwealth Prime Ministers' conferences and were held on a less formal basis than previously and also more frequently — roughly every two years.

India, Pakistan and Ceylon attended the 1948 conference so that they could see how the association worked at the highest level before taking a final decision about their own position. The following year saw discussion of India's wish to become a republic, and the communique recorded that the other members accepted this and recognised India's continued membership.

The growth of the Commonwealth produced strains which became evident in 1956. The conference of that year discussed the nationalisation by President Nasser of Egypt of the Suez Canal. However, some months later, in November, Britain joined France and Israel in an attack on Egypt without consulting or even informing her Commonwealth partners. The association might have been destroyed. The Canadian Foreign Minister, Mr. Lester Pearson, pronounced the Commonwealth on the verge of dissolution. The reaction in India was even more hostile. Mr. Nehru sent a formal protest to London — an unprecedented action for a Commonwealth country — and there were demands that India should leave the Commonwealth. Only Mr. (later Sir) Robert Menzies of Australia supported the British action. He commented: "It was — and I will say it if I am the only one left to say it — brave and correct".

Suez marked the beginning of a period in which Britain was to be increasingly criticised by her Commonwealth partners for real or imagined failures in policy — most of the new ones, after all, came from the Afro-Asian bloc and had a severe attitude to vestiges of colonialism. As a natural consequence there was a certain disenchantment with the whole idea of the Commonwealth in Britain itself, a disenchantment which has persisted to the present.

The conference of 1961 saw the character of the Commonwealth change again as the result of the departure of South Africa. The immediate cause was that the whites had voted in favour of republican status (the blacks didn't have a vote), and it became necessary for the South African government formally to apply for continued membership.

Other members, of course, had become republics and continued in the Commonwealth. But South Africa was a special case. Its government was carrying out a policy of apartheid, or separate development of the races, and this was in sharp contrast to the multi-racial aspirations of the Commonwealth. In the previous year there had been the massacre at Sharpeville in which police fired on unarmed African demonstrators, killing 67 of them and injuring 180.

By 1961 the Commonwealth had acquired several new non-European members, including one in Africa (Ghana). The racial policies of South Africa were therefore subjected to fierce scrutiny. One of the chief critics was the Canadian Prime Minister, Mr. John Diefenbaker, who was said to have presented his views with great emotion. A special communique issued before the end of the meeting recorded the result of the criticisms: "The Prime Minister of South Africa informed the other Prime Ministers this evening that in the light of the views expressed on behalf of other member governments and the indications of their future intentions regarding the racial policy of the Union government he had decided to withdraw his application for South Africa's continuing membership of the Commonwealth as a republic."

The wording is of some importance. South Africa was not expelled, as some people imagine; there is no machinery for expelling a member of the Commonwealth. It withdrew because it could no longer remain in an association fundamentally opposed to its internal policies. South Africa's Prime Minister, Dr. Verwoerd, said he had been amazed and shocked at the hostility shown to his country. He thought this marked the beginning of the disintegration of the Commonwealth. In one sense he was right. The old Commonwealth, in which white superiority was taken for granted, finally died on 15th March 1961 after languishing since 1948. In its place was the new Commonwealth, in which all races met in complete equality.

Most of the other leaders recognised this and argued that the withdrawal of South Africa would strengthen the association. Mrs. Bandaranaike of Ceylon, for example, saw it as "a dramatic vindication of the equality and human dignity for which the Commonwealth stands". Reaction in Britain was somewhat less enthusiastic. Mr. Macmillan, who had hoped to avoid the breach, expressed regret that circumstances had made this impossible. It is clear to us now, of course, that South Africa could not have stayed in the Commonwealth without destroying it.

The 1962 conference saw Britain under attack for wanting to join the European Economic Community, formed some years before. It was a decision taken after much heart searching. When the EEC was originally set up Britain held aloof. In public it was argued, among other things, that Commonwealth interests must be protected, but in practice no British government has ever put the interests of the Commonwealth as a whole before what it deems to be those of the nation. A more cogent reason was that the Foreign Office, in its wisdom, didn't think the EEC would, work; it could not imagine a group of European countries, including hereditary enemies, actually combining in an economic community.

When the British government under Mr. Macmillan decided in 1961 that the economic facts of life compelled Britain to throw in her lot with Europe, the Commonwealth was appalled. Ministers attending the Commonwealth Economic Consultative Council in Accra spoke of the grave apprehension and concern of the other members. By 1962 some of the shock had worn off, but even so there was considerable argument among the prime ministers who met in London. Communiques are generally intended to conceal differences, not to emphasise them, but the communique resulting from the 1962 conference admitted "many differences of viewpoint and many uncertainties". At the same time it was acknowledged that the final responsibility was that of the British government. That particular application was vetoed by General de Gaulle, but membership remained the aim of successive British governments, and when it was finally achieved in 1973 the Commonwealth had become reconciled to the fact. In 1975, just before the referendum on whether Britain should remain a member, Commonwealth leaders issued a statement saying they hoped she would.

Criticism of Britain by other members became a feature of the conferences during the 1960s; it focussed particularly on relations with southern Africa, notably Rhodesia. This was a self-governing colony, with its own armed forces, and when other African colonies were being given independence the Rhodesian government asked for it as well. There was, though, one big difference. Political and economic power was in the hands of the small white minority, and the British government refused to grant independence without constitutional safeguards for progress to majority rule. As early as 1964 this potential source of friction was noted by Commonwealth leaders.

It was also an issue in 1965, but this conference was diverted by a curious piece of political gamesmanship indulged in by the British Prime Minister, Sir Harold Wilson, then a commoner and at the beginning of his term of office. He had a small majority in the House of Commons, and his support for the American government in the Vietnam war was making some of his left-wing MPs restive. He proposed a Commonwealth peace mission to Vietnam — using the Commonwealth for his own political ends, some members complained. The mission was to consist of Wilson himself, the President of Ghana (Nkrumah) and the Prime Ministers of Nigeria and Trinidad. Its purpose was "to explore with the parties principally concerned how far there might be common ground about the circumstances in which a peace conference might be held".

This oddly constituted mission achieved nothing . It wasn't even able to visit Vietnam, and it sank without trace. Its failure underlined the fact that the Commonwealth could no longer be regarded as a major force in world affairs. Although a few leaders were prevailed on to join the mission, most viewed it with scepticism, and one, President Nyerere of Tanzania, disassociated himself from it completely. The membership was now too varied to present a common front to the world on any political topic on which there was controversy.

However, the conference showed that the Commonwealth, if it was politically impotent, had an important part to play in developing functional co-operation between its members. It approved the setting up of the Commonwealth Foundation to promote interchanges between the professions and the Commonwealth Secretariat as "a visible symbol of the spirit of co-operation which animates the Commonwealth". The first Secretary-General appointed was a Canadian diplomat, Mr. Arnold Smith. We shall be looking at both these bodies in more detail later. For the moment it is only necessary to make the point that the 1965 conference demonstrated clearly that the Commonwealth had undergone a metamorphosis — from chrysalis to butterfly, from a political to a functional association which would need to justify its existence not on the grounds of sentiment and common purpose, but on its degree of practical utility to its members.

But there was still one major political problem unsolved, and it was very much a Commonwealth problem. In November 1965 the white government of Rhodesia made its unilateral declaration of independence. The British government, which had ruled out the use of force in advance, imposed sanctions. Commonwealth leaders met in Lagos in January 1966 to discuss the Rhodesian crisis. The meeting broke new grounds in several ways. It was the first to be held outside London, the first to be organised by the new Secretariat and the first to be called to deal with a single issue. It achieved another and less happy distinction. A few days after it was over the host, Sir Abubakar Tafewa Balewa, Prime Minister of Nigeria, was assassinated in a military coup — the first of several the country was to undergo.

A number of Commonwealth leaders at the Lagos conference, advocated the use of force, but Harold Wilson argued that his expert advice was that sanctions might bring the rebellion to an end "in weeks rather than months". As the communique put it in a delightful understatement: "Some Prime Ministers had misgivings in this regard" — and well they might. The conference, though, had some positive results. It set up a programme for training Rhodesian Africans and also a Commonwealth committee to review the effect of sanctions. It also agreed that there should be another meeting in July if the rebellion had not been brought to an end by then.

It was not until September that this second meeting of the year was held — in London — and the rebellion was still flourishing. This meeting was perhaps the most fraught and potentially destructive ever held. Nine of the eleven days were devoted to Rhodesia. The African, Asian and Caribbean leaders formed a caucus, designed to bring pressure on the British government. The use of force was again argued, but the British said it simply wasn't possible; the Africans didn't believe them. Under all these pressures Mr. Wilson commented crossly: "We are getting a little tired of carrying the can internationally for a regime that has no regard for international opinions. We have had to pay a very heavy price for carrying that can in the last ten days. We have faced very serious dangers of the break-up of the Commonwealth because of the actions of a small group of men."

The Commonwealth did not, in fact, break up — its death, forecast for some time, was again postponed. A compromise of a sort was reached on Rhodesia. The British Government was permitted to make one last attempt to persuade the regime to accept independence with safeguards leading to majority rule. Failing that it was committed to the new doctrine of NIBMAR — No Independence Before Majority Rule.

By the time of the next conference, in 1969, the Rhodesian regime had rejected the attempt at a settlement. The issue was therefore debated all over again, but there was an improvement in the atmosphere. Since 1966 all the parties concerned had been able to reflect that the Commonwealth was too valuable to be destroyed by a temporary disagreement, however deep. Mr. Arnold Smith, too, had been active in mending fences. Some African leaders again argued for the use of force, but Mr. Wilson defended his policies towards Rhodesia, and, although most of the Prime Ministers disagreed with him, he was able to say at the end: "What has marked this conference has been the friendly, responsible, moderate, comradely way in which these disagreements have been expressed." He said it had been a very good conference: "Everything was discussed that could be inside or outside the conference, and I think that most of my colleagues, while inevitably they must express their disappointments about where they failed to move us, for example on Rhodesia, will feel that it is the best conference we have had." The Prime Minister of New Zealand, Keith Holyoake, agreed, describing the conference as one of the most constructive of recent years.

The Commonwealth might have entered a period of comparative tranquility after 1969, had it not been for a change of government in Britain. The Conservatives won the election of 1970, and a part of their programme was to reverse the arms embargo on South Africa to the extent of allowing the sale of frigates and other naval equipment. During the election campaign this was seldom mentioned. Elections are not fought nowadays on issues of foreign policy but on matters of more vital concern, such as which party is the more adept at encouraging two television sets to grow where one grew before.

Immediately after the election the *Guardian* newspaper, sensing a good campaigning issue, made much of the Conservative intention, and this initiated a fierce debate within the country, the Commonwealth and the continent of Africa. Several African leaders visited London and had well-publicised rows with the Prime Minister, Mr. Heath, President Kaunda of Zambia going as far as to say he had come to appeal to the British people over the head of their government.

Mr. Heath's argument was that the supply of certain items of equipment was legally required under the terms of the Simonstown Agreement of 1955, under which the Royal Navy received facilities at the Simonstown base in South Africa. (The Labour administration had maintained there was no such obligation.) In addition he pointed to the increase in Soviet naval activity in the Indian Ocean and the need for a trading nation such as Britain to protect the sea lanes. Opponents of his policy argued that would help the 'South African government to hold down their black population under a policy which was deeply immoral because it condemned black people to permanent second-class citizenship through a mere accident of birth.

The stage was thus set for a fierce argument at the next Commonwealth conference. This was held in Singapore in January 1971, the intention being to show that the Commonwealth was now a truly multilateral institution and no longer needed always to hold its deliberations in London. Mr. Heath took the offensive almost at once and lectured the others about the Commonwealth. It was a body of friends, he said, not a court of judgement, and it had no right to stop member goverments making their own decisions. The debate was prolonged — it extended at one point to an all-night sitting. The upshot was to appoint a study group to look into the question of the defence of the Indian Ocean, thus deferring the whole problem. The problem itself eventually disappeared in any case. The British government decided that its legal obligations to South Africa involved the sale only of seven helicopters. Nobody was prepared to make an issue of this — except to withdraw from the study group, which never met — and no further arms were sold. The end of the story might be regarded as a victory for the Commonwealth, whose pressures had induced Mr. Heath to modify his stand, although the decisive argument was probably the likelihood of losing trade with a number of African countries.

The Singapore conference was notable in other ways. As part of the strategy to prevent the British arms sales President Kaunda produced a draft declaration under which member governments were to subscribe to a number of principles, including a pledge not to give help to racialist regimes. After a good deal of argument this was modified to enable each country to be the judge of whether its own actions helped a

taken place in the world economic outlook — a huge rise in oil prices after the Arab-Israel war of October 1973, recession in the west and a sharpening of the confrontation between the developed and developing countries. In Jamaica ideas for changes in the world economic order were aired, criticised and finally put to a group of ten experts to produce a report. This is discussed in greater detail in the following chapter.

It had been thought that the next conference would be in Nairobi in 1977, but Commonwealth leaders accepted an invitation from Harold Wilson to hold it in London, because it would coincide with the silver jubilee of the Queen, who is, after all, head of the Commonwealth. Not everybody was happy with this decision, since it was held that the wrong idea might be created in the public mind — subjects of a far-flung empire come to pay homage to the Queen, as in Victorian times, perpetuating imperial myths.

In fact, these meetings are quite unlike anything which existed in Victorian times. Since many Commonwealth countries are Republics with their own executive presidents, they are known now as heads of government conferences rather than Prime Ministers' conferences. They continue to be held in private, although the opening ceremony is now televised, and they remain comparatively informal. In Jamaica the practice was that certain heads of government made prepared keynote speeches on particular topics, and for the rest the discussion was general. Actually, so many of them spoke for so long that a time limit of ten minutes apiece had to be imposed.

In Ottawa and again in Jamaica the convention was established of all the Commonwealth leaders retiring *en masse* for the weekend to a plushy country retreat, where they could play golf or ride horses or just sit around and chat. Their more formal deliberations in the conference chamber are covered by certain conventions which are longer established. They do not, except with permission, discuss each other's internal affairs. They do not vote; they seek consensus, but if it is lacking they agree to disagree. They do not confine themselves to Commonwealth matters. They discuss world political and economic trends in general, each contributing from his or her experience. They also discuss, but not so you would notice, the specifically Commonwealth programmes which operate under their auspices. These programmes are what this book is mainly about; they are generally regarded as one of the chief justifications of the Commonwealth, but, since they are uncontroversial, the heads of government normally dispose of them in less than half a day.

The conferences, which used to last about ten days, have recently been getting shorter. It is, after all, a good deal to ask busy statesmen from all over the world to come together and talk about all manner of subjects which are not always of immediate concern and about which, in any case, they are not normally expected to take decisions. So what makes them do it? Aren't they simply wasting their own time and that of everybody else connected with the meetings?

One reason they attend, of course, is the simple desire to travel and meet people. The leaders of the smaller Commonwealth countries in particular receive a boost to their prestige by mixing on equal and familiar terms with statesmen of international repute. There is also domestic public opinion to be considered. A politician can gain considerable support from the people back home by being presented in the press as having stood firm in his country's interests at an international gathering such as a Commonwealth conference — a lesson British Prime Ministers are particularly quick to learn.

But these are the views of a cynical outsider. The politicians themselves express it rather differently, as in these remarks by the Canadian Prime Minister, Mr. Pierre Trudeau after the Ottawa conference: "We shall be asked by our electorates what we did this past week, asked what we accomplished. We talked, we will tell them. We sought and gained a greater understanding of the position of one another. We agreed again and again . . . that we should seek constructive solutions. We came to know one another better, and all of us regard this as good — good for now and good for the future, good for us as leaders and good for our peoples."

That Mr. Trudeau should express himself so positively is of some significance, since he has confessed that when he came to power some years earlier he was sceptical of the value of the Commonwealth, regarding it as an anachronism. After being involved in its work he became (in his own words) a "deep convert". What better way to end this chapter than with the philosophy of a "deep convert"?

"These Commonwealth conferences are distinctive for two

reasons. . . . The first is the obvious dedication of Commonwealth leaders to the betterment of their peoples. Not here are there propounded or vigorously defended schemes or programmes designed for the glory of the state. Here we are concerned with the dignity of individual human beings and the improvement of the lot of ordinary men and women.

"The second distinction is a willingness on the part of all of us to believe that should the policies of other Commonwealth governments sometimes appear misdirected or lead to disappointment this is as a result of error or ineffiiency or lack of discipline; it is not the consequence of purposeful intent.

"In short, within the Commonwealth there is a willingness to help one another and a willingness to believe that that help is genuinely offered.

"Given those beliefs, this association is far different from those others to which we belong in various groupings. Here we are able to speak to one another with a candour unknown elsewhere. We are not reluctant to describe our individual weaknesses, our dreams for our peoples, our belief in the value of human life, our dedication to the concepts of co-operation and understanding. We are not fearful of admitting that we do not know all the answers, that our ignorance has led to mistakes, that our patience with ourselves and with one another is sometimes sorely tried.

"We find value in gathering together periodically because we believe there is merit in candid talk. There is no other forum available for this purpose for political decision-makers from all parts of the world. And certainly none where we all speak the same language."

CHAPTER THREE

Life At The Hub

The Secretariat, the hub of the Commonwealth, is located in Marlborough House, just off Pall Mall in London. This is a royal residence — it was once the home of Queen Mary, the widow of George V — and is used as a centre for the Commonwealth with the blessing of the Queen. Its splendid reception rooms are still used for occasional social functions and also for constitutional conferences leading to independence for Britain's few remaining colonies.

There are those who regret the choice of site, on the grounds that it serves to keep alive the erroneous idea that Britain is still the centre of the Commonwealtth. There is a good deal in this argument. but in terms of practical efficiency it is difficult to suggest where else it might be, at least for the present. London is the only capital where every Commonwealth country has a diplomatic mission, it has good communications, and it is the headquarters of most of the numerous unofficial Commonwealth organisations.

At the same time, most people in Britain assume that the Secretariat is a British government organisation — a misapprehension which exists even among those who should know better — MPs and senior civil servants, for example. In fact, it is multi-national. It is at the service of all Commonwealth governments, and all of them contribute to its cost in proportion to their size and wealth. Its first Secretary-General was a Canadian, and he was succeeded by a Guyanese.

Its senior staff serve for limited periods — there is no lifetime career in the Secretariat — so it is difficult to say exactly which countries are represented at any given time. But the memorandum under which it was set up in 1965 made the point that staff should be recruited on as wide a geographical basis as possible, and most of the member countries are represented.

A researcher from Canada who spent some time in the Secretariat in 1974 made the following observations: "This pot-pourri of nationalities blends more easily because of the existence of English as a common working language. The fact that oral and written commication difficulties are few is an inestimable advantage not only to the Secretariat but also to the Commonwealth as a whole. . . .

"But the Secretariat not only benefits from a common working language but also from what may be called a common 'style'. Style is an elusive quality, but it is one which most senior members of the Secretariat tended to stress in personal interviews, and for that reason alone it is worth trying to capture some of its meaning. It has, of course, nothing to do with that kind of panache which admirers have attributed to the Kennedy administration of the early 1960s; there is no flavour of Camelot about Marlborough House. Commonwealth style, which probably derives in the main from comparable education and administrative experience, is perhaps a way of looking at problems and a recognisable approach to dealing with them. It deals in common sense rather than political rhetoric, prefers informality to protocol and performance to theory. Described thus (and imperfectly) it may sound the antithesis of style: low-key, pragmatic, sensible."[1]

The author also found that "there was general consensus among senior staff that it was doing a useful job, and this was a refreshing attitude to encounter amoung members of an international bureaucracy".

The memorandum setting up the Secretariat made it clear that "it should operate initially on a modest footing" and should not arrogate to itself executive functions. Behind this lay the fear — familiar from 60 years earlier — that it might become too powerful and try to take over wide powers. It was, after all, the first time the Commonwealth had been institutionalised, and the heads of government were nervous of their own creation.

Mr. Smith, therefore, began his career as Secretary-General with a handful of staff and the knowledge that his freedom of action was

(1) *The Commonwealth Secretariat* by Margaret Doxey (Year Book of World Affairs, 1976).

limited. But he had a number of advantages; he was an experienced diplomat, with a belief in the Commonwealth, and he had direct access to the heads of government. The post was regarded as the equivalent of a senior High Commissioner.[2] Under his leadership the Secretariat became accepted by Commonwealth leaders, who piled an increasing number of tasks on it, and it even played a modest diplomatic role — for example, bringing together the two sides in the Nigerian civil war, albeit briefly. Mr. Smith was re-appointed for a second five-year term in 1970. He was succeeded in 1975 by Mr. Shridath ('Sonny') Ramphal, the Foreign Minister of Guyana.

The growth of the Secretariat during these years has been impressive. It began with two functional divisions — international affairs and economic — together with an administrative unit. Before long it had taken over the Commonwealth Education Liaison Unit (established 1959) and the Commonwealth Economic Committee (1925) as an education division and commodities division respectively. A scientific adviser was also appointed. Later came a medical adviser (1968), a legal division (1969), an information division (1971), a fund for technical co-operation (1971), a youth division (1973), a division for applied studies in government (1975) and a food production and rural development division (1975). By 1976 the staff had grown to over three hundred and the budget to some two million pounds a year.[3]

This growth was not the result of Parkinson's Law but arose from the demands made on the Secretariat at various ministerial meetings, including those of the heads of government. Like the Commonwealth itself, it was unplanned; the Secretariat was, as it were, made up as it went along.

One factor in this was the growth in membership of the Commonwealth itself. In 1965 there were 21 fully independent members, ten years later there were 35. Most of the new members were small, economically weak states which looked for help in their development. They saw an important source for this help in the Commonwealth. This

(2) Commonwealth countries exchange High Commissioners, not Ambassadors. Their functions are much the same, but they have certain privileges of access to ministers and, of course, they have the language in common.

(3) For comparison, the budget for the United Nations, not including the specialised agencies, amounted to about £370 million in 1976-77.

it might be as well to try to describe roughly what it means.[4]

It is based on the premise that the existing system of world trade and finance is an inheritance from the days of empire and therefore heavily weighted in favour of the industrialised powers. One effect of this has been graphically illustrated by several Commonwealth leaders, among them Mr. Michael Manley of Jamaica. He told the Ottawa conference that, if ten years ago his country could buy a tractor by selling ten tons of sugar, it now cost fifty tons of sugar to buy the same tractor. Inflation in the industrialised countries, in fact, was not matched by rises in commodity prices. "We're all trapped in this thing," he said. "It's like trying to walk up the down escalator."

The moves to alter this state of affairs have come from various meetings of non-aligned nations and the so-called Group of 77 — they now number over 100 — developing nations which have formed a bloc within the United Nations. (The countries involved in the two groups are largely the same; they are meeting under different hats.) For example, in 1970 the summit meeting of non-aligned nations in Lusaka, Zambia, adopted a declaration which said in part: "the persistence of an inequitable world economic system inherited from the colonial past and continued through present-day neo-colonialism poses insurmountable difficulties in breaking the bondage of poverty and economic dependence."

A similar point was made rather more picturesquely and without jargon by an Iranian official after a meeting of the Organisation of Petroleum Exporting Countries. "It's time," he said, "to change the idea that people with blonde hair and blue eyes run the world, and people with dark hair and dark eyes should knock on the back door."

The cause received enormous encouragement from the quadrupling of prices by the OPEC countries after the Middle East war of 1973; for the first time producers had been able to fix their own prices instead of having them imposed by what the consumers thought the market would bear. Although many developing countries were severely hit by the rise in oil prices, they did not break ranks with the oil producers; together they produced a programme for action in making far-

(4) The New International Economic Order with initial capital letters refers, strictly speaking, to the proposals emanating from the Sixth Special Session of the United Nations Assembly. I am using the term in a slightly more general sense.

reaching changes in the world economic system which they pressed at the Sixth Special Session of the United Nations Assembly in 1974.

Among the principles laid down at this meeting were "a just and equitable" relationship between the prices of imports and exports of developing countries, support for associations of producers ("cartels" in American demonology), regulation of multi-national (transnational) companies, increased economic aid and access by the developing countries to the achievements of science and technology. (Later came a call for "indexation" — that is, linking the price of commodities to those of manufactured goods so as to compensate the producers for inflation in the industrialised world.) The declaration was passed without a vote, but the industrialised countries regarded the programme as extreme and had considerable reservations.

An attempt to open a dialogue between the two sides in Paris in April 1975 failed because the industrialised countries wanted to confine the discussions to energy problems, while the developing countries wanted a whole range of other economic questions on the agenda. The atmosphere, in fact, was almost as bad as it could be. The so-called "North-South" dialogue seemed to have broken off before it had begun.[5]

This was the background against which the Commonwealth heads of government conference was held in Kingston, Jamaica, in May 1975. It was known beforehand that the question of the world economic order would be an important topic at the conference. The Commonwealth seemed a suitable forum. It included an important oil producer (Nigeria), several industrialised nations, including a major importer of raw materials (Britain), a number of countries which depend heavily on the export of commodities, or in some cases a single commodity. It also contains countries with a foot in both camps — Australia and Canada, for example, which are industrial countries but also important commodity producers.

In the event the conference witnessed two contrasting attitudes. The British Prime Minister, Harold Wilson, came armed with what he himself described as an important initiative on commodities, based on

(5) Most industrialised countries are in the northern hemisphere — North America, Europe, Japan. Most of the poorer ones are to the south of them , if not actually in the southern hemisphere. Hence the North-South equation.

the principle "that the wealth of the world must be redistributed in favour of the poverty stricken and starving." He proposed a General Agreement on Commodities, on the lines of the General Agreement on Tariffs and Trade (GATT) of a generation earlier, together with a series of individual commodity agreements (between producers and consumers) and arrangements for stabilising export earnings of commodity producers by compensating them for falls in world prices.

Mr. Forbes Burnham of Guyana, speaking on behalf of the Caribbean countries generally, dismissed these proposals as being out of date — based on arrangements made in the mid-fifties. "The proposals which Harold has made with respect to commodity arrangements do not match the objectives which he and his government have set themselves," was his comment. He argued that far more radical steps were needed and suggested that a group of Commonwealth experts should be set up to look into possible practical measures to bring about an economic order which would redistribute the world's wealth in favour of the poorer countries. This idea was accepted by the conference, the British proposals being among those to be considered by the group.

Ten experts were chosen, to serve in their personal capacities, not as representatives of their governments. They came from New Zealand, Bangladesh, Tanzania, Malaysia, Zambia, Britain, India, Nigeria and Canada, and the chairman was the Secretary-General of the Caribbean Community. They were serviced by the Secretariat. By August they had produced an interim report which was submitted to Commonwealth Finance Ministers, meeting in Georgetown, Guyana.

The report said that fundamental changes were needed in the world economy, not case-by-case adjustments of an essentially marginal character. A substantially different structure of international economic relations was required. It advocated indexation as an important element in commodity agreements and supported producer associations. As for a General Agreement on Commodities, it "could be of value at an appropriate stage".

In general, then, the report favoured the arguments put forward by the developing countries, and not all its suggestions found favour with the finance ministers from the industrialised members of the Commonwealth, such as Britain. Nevertheless, it went forward to the Seventh General Session of the United Nations Assembly and probably helped to contribute to the cordiality of that gathering — at least, as compared with the session of the previous year.

However, the expert group was not finished. It met again and produced a second report looking in more detail at certain problems, notably commodity arrangements, the debt burdens of developing countries and industrial development. Its final report was presented to the heads of Government conference in 1977.

Of course, the Commonwealth is not alone in the search for a new international economic order. It is being pursued — and resisted — in a large number of international settings. But the Commonwealth is a cross-section of humanity, and its discussions are carried on more easily and informally than most. It seems particularly well suited to contribute, and the Secretariat will have a key role to play.

But it is likely to be a long-drawn-out process. For one thing, the rich have never in history shown much disposition to alter voluntarily a system which made them rich in the first place. For another, the cause isn't helped by the fact that many Third World countries have governments which are corrupt, inefficient or tyrannical (or all three) and show enormous contrasts of wealth and poverty within their own borders. This is not true of all of them, and, in any case, is not the fault of their people. But it does make public opinion in the industrialised world sceptical of the value of trying to help them.

However, public opinion isn't immutable. When President Nyerere of Tanzania visited Britain in 1975 he made a speech in which he pleaded eloquently for a just economic order, arguing: "We are poor because you are rich".

There came a voice from the audience: "Are you asking the hard-pressed British taxpayer to dig in his pocket even deeper to help you?"

President Nyerere didn't try to prevaricate or argue. He replied simply: "Yes."

And the rest of the audience — mostly hard-pressed British taxpayers themselves — burst into a storm of applause.

CHAPTER FOUR

Economic And Technical Co-operation

The demand for a a new international economic order was in part a reaction to the failure of international development aid to do enough to raise the living standards of the poor. Successive "Development Decades" proclaimed by the United Nations produced disillusion rather than development, mainly because the aid-giving countries did not devote enough of their resources to them — on average a good deal less than one per cent of their total wealth, as measured in terms of gross national product. In addition, the type of aid — mostly based on Western technology — may not always have been appropriate.

But it is worth remembering that the idea of economic aid — the voluntary transfer of real resources from the rich countries to the poor — is less than 30 years old. Although the British government gave some financial help to its dependencies as long ago as 1929, aid began as a major activity only after the last war. Two Commonwealth aid organisations — the Commonwealth Development Corporation and the Colombo Plan — date from that era.

The Development Corporation, in spite of its name, is a purely British organisation. It was set up as a statutory corporation in 1948 to help in the economic development of British colonies. It was empowered to borrow from the government and required to show a return on its investments. In its early days the Corporation ran into serious difficulties and had to abandon many of the projects in which it had invested. In the words of its official historian: "The board was prepared under strong political pressure to follow a policy of headlong expansion, which in the event was found to have taken insufficient

36

concerned in this question. Many of them are young, many committ
Christians, many members of the various voluntary organisations, sɪ
as Oxfam. War On Want, Save The Children Fund and others. Toget
they form a pressure-group — the "aid lobby" — which works at trɪ
to persuade both official and public opinion of the need for greɪ
efforts. They have allies in the government itself, in the Minist
Overseas Development, which is responsible for administering th
programme. And they have some academics on their side, in the
of such bodies as the Overseas Development Institute, an indepe
research and information body, and the Institute of Develo
Studies at Sussex University.

The facts about British aid are easy enough to find for a
who cares to look for them. For the financial year 1976-77 t
which was expected to be spent was something over £500 milli
is less than four-tenths of one per cent (0.4) of the countr
wealth, as expressed in terms of gross national product. This i
case of throwing huge sums of money about; in fact, meas
proportion of Britain's total public expenditure, aid has beeɪ
ing steadily since the early 1960s.

It is commonly supposed in Britain that aid money goes
corrupt politicians in Third World countries who buy ther
vate yachts and other luxuries and live a life of slothful
expense of the taxpayer. This is the concept attacked as "
rich countries helping the rich in poor countries". Th
element of truth in it, in the sense that Western aid gener
of its relatively sophisticated nature, has tended to bene
off rather than the mass of the people. But, although th
abuses in the past, it is not true in the sense that indi
unduly. Aid funds are given for specific projects, like ɪ
and there are stringent controls over actual disburseɪ

In any case, the British, in common with many oʲ
have decided to put the emphasis in their aid progran
the very poorest people in the poorest countries. Thɪ
tries where the average income per head is two hund
or less, and (as we saw in Chapter Three) many oʲ
Commonwealth. The poorest people mostly live in
emphasis becomes one of encouraging rural develoʲ

---

regard to the need first to build up an adequate management structure."[1]

For those with long enough memories, the Corporation has been
associated with the failure of a scheme to grow groundnuts in what was
then Tanganyika. But this is a myth. It was the Overseas Food Corporation (later wound up) which was responsible for that developmental
failure in the early post-war years. However, the CDC has its own
spectacular blunders, including a scheme for the production of eggs in
The Gambia. In 1950 Lord Reith, the forbidding Scot who had built up
the BBC, was appointed chairman of the Corporation. He carried out a
drastic reorganisation and put it on its feet.

Its terms of reference were changed in 1963 — after a long battle
— to enable it to operate in former colonies which had become
independent. But, since India, Pakistan and Sri Lanka (Ceylon) had
achieved independence before it was formed, it has never been active
in those countries. Since 1969 it has been empowered to take part in
projects in certain countries outside the Commonwealth. Its main
spheres of operation are in the Caribbean, Africa, South-east Asia and
the Pacific. It invests in projects by itself or in partnership with governmental or private concerns. Although it is meant to show a profit, the
first criterion is that of need. It goes in for a wide variety of projects.
Here are a few of them:

An irrigation scheme in Swaziland, together with associated
agricultural projects;
Smallholders' schemes for growing tea in Kenya, Uganda and
Malawi;
Cement factories in Zambia and Nigeria;
Cattle ranches in Botswana;
Mortgage finance companies in Malaysia and many Caribbean
countries;
Tourist hotels in the Caribbean.
The CDC pioneered what is called the nucleus estate. This is a
plantation run on commercial lines with a smallholders' scheme next to
it. The advantage is that the plantation management can help the
smallholder by practical demonstrations and technical advice, train his

managers and help to market his crops. In the words o
history: "In CDC experience nucleus estates performed
function, and the Corporation liked to think that the
resented a distinctive CDC contribution to developmen

The CDC also provides a unique service in that its p
management, where necessary, and this includes the t
people to take over as managers. It is now concentrati
rural development, in accordance with the British g
programme. For (to repeat) it is purely British, altho
have been made from time to time that it should
Commonwealth agency, with contributions from oth
as Canada or Australia.

The British aid programme itself is largely dev
monwealth; 80 per cent of British aid goes to Con
tries, for reasons of history and also of convenienc
and techniques — even slang terms — are familia
wealth countries.

The aid programme is often attacked in Brit
pletely opposite viewpoints. There are those wh
more accurate, feel — that the country shouldn'
money to wicked and ungrateful foreigners wh
make ends meet ("the hard-pressed British tax
often expressed by the more chauvinistic newspa
tedly held by a large number of people who
compassion if they witnessed a child — or, fo
being ill-treated or neglected. There are vai
other side, including those of both morality
reason doesn't have much influence on thinki
question of having the imagination to see that
would be untold wealth to millions in the T

On the extreme left, aid programmes ar
the argument being that they ensure that th
held in thrall by the industrialised countrie
some cases, but the fact is that Third W
mostly complain that the trouble with eco
enough of it.

This is also a view held by those in I

encouraging people to stay on the land, instead of drifting to the cities, which means in turn improving the quality of their lives. Roads, schools, hospitals, clinics, water and power supplies, all these and many more, are the requirements included under the heading of rural development.

Britain is the main supplier of capital aid in the Commonwealth, but there are others, including Canada, Australia, New Zealand and Nigeria. In addition, the other member countries play their part in the Colombo Plan or the Commonwealth Fund for Technical Co-operation (or both).

The Colombo Plan, although it now extends far beyond the Commonwealth, was in its conception a Commonwealth initiative. This was in 1950, when Commonwealth Foreign Ministers were meeting in Colombo. The original idea came from the representatives of Australia and Ceylon (now Sri Lanka), and it was endorsed by ministers from five other countries — Britain, Canada, India, New Zealand and Pakistan.

It was a time when Marshall Aid was helping the war-ravaged countries of Europe, and some urgent action was held to be needed to help the newly-independent countries of southern Asia. The plan drawn up at the Colombo meeting came into effect 18 months later with the title "The Colombo Plan for Co-operative Economic Development in South and South-East Asia". The use of the word "co-operative" in this lengthy title has a good deal of significance. The Plan's slogan is "Planning Prosperity Together", and the intention has always been for all the countries of the region to contribute their skills, not simply to accept aid from outside. To quote one of its own publications: "The driving force is provided by all the member countries . . . the hard work, hard thinking and sacrifice that are needed to turn paper plans into irrigation schemes and factories, roads and railways are provided almost entirely by the peoples of the region."

Since its inception a large number of other countries have joined the Plan. They are from outside the region — the United States, Canada and Japan, for example — and from inside. Regional membership now extends from Iran in the west to the Philippines and Fiji in the east and South Korea in the north. The institution, though, retains aspects of the Commonwealth which gave it birth. The annual ministerial meetings do not take votes but try to reach a consensus, and the Plan itself is difficult to define.

It is not actually an aid-giving body at all. Aid is negotiated direct between individual governments. What the Colombo Plan does is offer consultations between the members through its annual ministerial meetings and through a Council for Technical Co-operation. Technical co-operation provides an example of two of the principles on which the Plan was founded — self-help and mutual co-operation. A number of training institutions have been established in countries of the region and provide places for trainees from all over the Plan area. In addition, students have been to countries outside the region.

Another — and newer — source of technical aid is the Commonwealth Fund for Technical Co-operation (CFTC). This is one of the almost unknown success stories of Commonwealth co-operation, which is valued by all the developing member countries for the speed and flexibility with which it operates. It began in 1971 with resources of only £400,000. By the financial year 1976–77 this had risen to seven million pounds.

It is a voluntary scheme to which all the Commonwealth governments now, in fact, subscribe, although Australia stayed aloof at the beginning. It is administered by the Commonwealth Secretariat, although it is funded separately. It provides advice, experts and training facilities to all member states and also to those which are still dependencies or in the halfway stage known as associated states (mostly small islands in the Caribbean).

Here is an official account of its operations: "The CFTC is not a traditional aid-giving agency operated by the wealthier nations, but a co-operative endeavour among all its members. Its management structure and its method of financing are devised to match this aim . The Fund's resources are subscribed by annual contributions, in convertible or non-convertible currency. The largest contributors are Canada, Britain, Australia, Nigeria, and New Zealand; the Canadian arrangement for matching on a two-for-one basis the contributions from developing members up to a given ceiling figure each year, and the British arrangement to provide 30 per cent of total expenditure, also up to a stated ceiling, offer an incentive to developing countries to increase their contributions.

"General policy is formulated by the Board of Representatives with one member from each participating country. The Board meets twice a year, one of its meetings normally being held in conjunction with the annual meeting of Commonwealth Finance Ministers. A small committee of management of 12 members, with the Commonwealth Secretary-General as chairman, meets more frequently to provide detailed policy guidance."

In the few years of its existence the CFTC has met some urgent high-level requests. In one Commonwealth country the Chinese built an excellent textile mill, but, in accordance with their usual practice, didn't provide a manager for it. The Prime Minister approached the Secretariat, the CFTC found a manager, and the mill went into operation on completion. The President of another country found that his post and telegraph service, which used to make a profit, was making serious losses; there was clearly something wrong. An urgent letter went to London, and out came a consultant, provided by the CFTC, who discovered the failings and made a number of recommendations which were put into effect.

Of course, requests don't usually come from Presidents and Prime Ministers but from rather lower down. The range of the Fund's activities is enormously varied and so is its geographical spread — from Antigua to Zambia, taking in most of the other Commonwealth countries on the way. It has three main spheres of activity: providing experts, providing training and providing help in finding export markets.

The experts come in all sorts of specialities and from all sorts of countries. Here, for instance, is a sample of what was going on under CFTC auspices during the last half of 1975: an economic adviser from Canada was in the Bahamas, a consultancy firm from Britain was making a study of deep coal mining in Bangladesh, a statistician from Sri Lanka was working in Fiji, an Indian was advising on tourism in The Gambia, a forensic pathologist from Bangladesh was operating in Guyana, a New Zealander was reviewing company legislation in Malawi, a Malaysian was advising on dairy goat production in Monserrat. And a little later a Jamaican was in the Gilbert Islands — soon to be independent — advising on setting up a small defence force with an additional developmental role.

These few examples are only a fraction of the Fund's activities in what is known as general technical assistance, but they give some idea of their criss-cross nature. It is very definitely not a case simply of experts going out from the developed countries. All the members are contributing, in expertise as well as money.

One of the advantages of the CFTC is that it works faster than other technical co-operation agencies. The time which elapses between receiving a request and having an expert on the spot is up to nine months, although sometimes it can be done more quickly. This is about half the average time taken by the United Nations Development Programme, and the main reason is the comparative lack of red tape.

The Fund, which operates from the Secretariat headquarters in Marlborough House, maintains a roster of about 3000 people in all parts of the Commonwealth who have a particular skill. Sometimes when the request is for something unusual — a speech therapist, for example — it seeks advice from outside bodies or even advertises. The time taken to fulfil a request depends on a number of factors, not all under the control of the Fund. Likely people have to be approached and their personal details sent to the government which is asking for the service. The government then lists them in order of preference — this may take some time — and then the question arises of how early the chosen individual can be released from his ordinary job, if only for a matter of weeks or months.

The weakness of this approach is that the Fund, which has no regional offices but operates entirely from London, does not always have first-hand knowledge of the individual concerned. This has sometimes led to difficulties. In one case an expert recruited by the Fund had to be withdrawn because he set himself up in business and spent most of his time competing for government contracts for his own benefit. In another case one member of a small team was continually complaining about his pay and status and made life so difficult for his colleagues — and the government which was using his services — that he had to be withdrawn.

A feature of the Fund is a small "fire brigade" unit — the Technical Assistance Group — based in London and ready to go to any part of the Commonwealth at short notice. It consists of a development economist, a lawyer, a taxation expert and a fiscal expert, and other skills can be added if necessary. They operate either individually or as a team. The group had a spectacular success in helping the government of Papua New Guinea, the former Australian trust territory which became independent in 1975. Before independence, the government wanted to negotiate better royalty terms with a large multi-national company, Rio-Tinto Zinc, which operates a copper mine on the island of Bougainville. But it didn't have the necessary experts of its own and was too poor to hire any. So it turned to the Commonwealth, and the Technical Assistance Group provided a team which was able to match the expertise of the company and produce a vastly improved agreement on royalties.

The CFTC generally has had a major programme of technical assistance to Papua New Guinea. It provided advice on the constitution, the relationship between the central and provincial governments, customary land legislation and law reform. It also provided a Supreme Court Judge.

In the education and training programme the emphasis has been on training in agriculture and the development of natural resources. But many other activities have been covered as well. People from some of the smaller Caribbean territories have been sent on hotel management courses at a training college in the Bahamas. From the island of Dominica a prison officer went to attend a course in Jamaica. Three people from Malawi were sent to Malaysia to study telecommunications engineering and two from the New Hebrides (jointly governed by Britain and France) to Fiji for a radio technicians' course. A student from Sierra Leone did a year of training in diplomacy at the University of Nairobi. And, perhaps the most unusual of all, two members of the staff of the Singapore zoo had an attachment of three months to the zoological gardens in Sri Lanka. The subject — elephant handling.

As for help with exports, to bring in badly needed foreign exchange, this is likely to be a part of the work of the CFTC which will grow. It has already had success in helping with the organisation of trade fairs for India (in Britain and the United States) and Malaysia (in Britain). The CFTC financed such services as market research and the identification of buyers. The India trade fair in New York was particularly well received. The buyers were astonished at the range of Indian goods available — not just traditional handicrafts but also modern industrial equipment at competitive prices. For an outlay by the Fund of about 200 000 dollars, the Indians earned 10½ million dollars in firm orders.

The CFTC doesn't automatically agree to every project suggested. Sometimes it turns them down because it seems already rather heavily committed to the particular country concerned, sometimes because it does not regard the project as sufficiently related to development, sometimes because it simply thinks it is wrong-headed. However, in the last case, which is not common, the Fund will usually try to work with the government to modify the project so that it makes more sense. And, of course, it is in a different position to other agencies for technical co-operation. All the Commonwealth governments subscribe to it, so all its customers are also its paymasters.

This fact, together with its low overheads and speed of response, makes the Commonwealth Fund for Technical Co-operation a unique institution providing for urgent, often small-scale, needs which are outside the scope of any other agency. And, judging by the enormous increase in its activities in the few years of its existence, Commonwealth countries place a high value on its work.

CHAPTER FIVE

Accent On Youth

In India engineering students got news of an earthquake, designed a shockproof school, then went to the devastated area and built a prototype. In Canada a group of young people created an urban community project, financing it by means of a farm in the country. In Zambia a youth group raised the money to build and operate a co-operative nutrition centre.

These are a few of the initiatives by young people which have received recognition under the Commonwealth Youth Programme, set up in 1973 with a pledge from Commonwealth governments of £1 million for its first three years. A review at the end of that time (1976) recommended that in future the programme should receive £1 million each year and that certain of its features should be changed.

Why a youth programme at all? Sixty per cent of the total population of the Commonwealth is under 25. Most of these young people live in countries where their opportunities for education and jobs are limited, even non-existent.

The problems they pose were outlined by the Secretary-General, Mr. Ramphal, when he spoke at a meeting of the Commonwealth Youth Affairs Council in Malta in April 1976: "There is increasing concern that the social values of the young are not properly understood and sympathetically acknowledged. Rising population figures highlight the probability of enlarged unemployment and its implications for the further deprivation of youth. The by-products of enforced leisure, if it can be called leisure — drug taking, alcoholism, violence, racial and community tensions — are inevitably causing grave concern to governments, given their social and political implications."

The aim of the Commonwealth Youth Programme is to encourage

46

young people to contribute to national development. It is administered by the youth division of the Secretariat under the guidance of the Commonwealth Youth Affairs Council, representing all the member governments. It has several main strands — youth development centres, Commonwealth youth projects, study fellowships and bursaries, a youth information service and support for national youth programmes.

There are three youth development centres — a new name for what were originally called regional centres for advanced youth work. They are in Guyana, Zambia and India. Each has its own regional flavour, but students from all over the Commonwealth may apply to attend courses at any of them. What they offer is a series of courses and seminars for youth workers. One aim is to help them to progress to a point where they can themselves become responsible for starting and developing training courses in their own countries and play a constructive part in national youth programmes. The review of the youth programme in 1976 recommended that courses at these centres should be more closely geared to the needs of the developing countries and rather less academic in nature.

This is a view which had already been expressed by some of those who attended the courses. For example, the first batch of graduates at the centre in Guyana came up with some constructive suggestions. The emphasis, they said, should be on practical skills. One student commented: "We would like to have more opportunities for field activities, especially in group work and youth projects."

Many of the students saw the centre as providing a back-up service once they had returned home. Others said they had gained much deeper insights and understanding both of themselves and others as a result of the course and had been helped by meeting youth workers from other countries.

Who attends these courses? Here is a profile of one of those who graduated from the centre in Guyana a few years ago to typify all the many others:

Basil Byer from Barbados had been apprenticed to a car mechanic, then became a teacher in a primary school, then an accounts clerk with a hire purchase firm, where he earned more money. At school he helped to form a cultural club, which continued as an old scholars association after he and the other founders left school. On the strength of this he was chosen for a course in social welfare by the Ministry of Education, and he became a community development officer, one of eight in Barbados.

In July 1974 he was accepted by the Commonwealth Youth Programme for the new course on youth studies at the Guyana centre. After eight weeks of intensive study there he returned to Barbados and began a field assignment, choosing as his special subject a community centre which caters for 100 young people. In July 1975 he went back to Guyana for ten weeks follow-up work. He graduated in September and went back to the Ministry of Education in Barbados, complete with a youth work diploma. He has no doubts about the value of his studies to the work he does in Barbados.

One of the most imaginative aspects of the youth programme as originally envisaged was the youth service awards as a recognition of outstanding achievements in the field of community service by youth groups. The idea was that Commonwealth governments should nominate up to three projects each year, to be judged by a special international panel. The teams involved in the best two projects were given the opportunity to travel to other Commonwealth countries to study youth activities and pass on their own experiences. The scheme has now been modified, and the judging panel has been dropped. Governments may now simply apply for travel fellowships for projects which they think might benefit.

The scheme has given recognition to some remarkable achievements. For example, some years ago young people in Kelantan in peninsular Malaysia had few jobs and not much income. Some had been to school for a period, others had no schooling. Their future seemed grim. Today the picture has changed, thanks to the club they established — the 4B Kasar Youth Club. It has more than 200 members, over half of them girls. They grow crops, rear poultry and breed cattle. To raise .funds they take up government contracts for road repairs and building construction in the area. And they conduct literacy classes for both adults and young prople. The 4B Kasar Youth Club was one of the first award winners under the scheme, and five of its members visited Ghana and The Gambia, where they met young people and studied projects similar to their own.

The other winner in that year (1974) was a club of a very different type — Cool Aid in Victoria, British Columbia. This was a group of young people who looked at the city's lack of facilities and set about solving the problem in their own way. They came up against opposition, and a good deal of apathy, but they established a home for homeless teenagers, a child day care centre, a theatre and a community centre, a dental and medical clinic and a 24-hour counselling service. To finance all this they ran a farm in the country. Under the Commonwealth scheme they were able to send a team to Australia and Hong Kong to study projects similar to their own.

In the following year the awards went to an Australian project, Women's Halfway House, which caters for the needs of the homeless, and to an Indian scheme of sending student volunteers to help in rural areas. In addition several cash awards were made. They went to help a youth club in The Gambia build a rural health centre, to a young people's welfare service in the Bahamas, to a polytechnic in Tanzania to set up a tin-smithing and mechanics' workshop and to young farmers in Ghana.

While awards are made to clubs, the bursaries and fellowships scheme is for individuals. The fellowships are awarded for short, intensive study trips to other Commonwealth countries by youth workers. The idea is that they will gain from sharing experience, exchanging ideas and adapting other peoples' solutions to their own problems.

A few examples of the fellowship scheme: A Bahamian has studied the youth service in Kenya and Ghana, a Fijian has examined community programmes for young women in India, a British West Indian community worker has been to the Caribbean, and youth workers from Guyana have been to Tanzania to study its system of national service.

Bursaries are intended for youth workers to undertake advanced training of what is described as "a profound and concentrated nature". They are confined to those attending courses at one of the three regional youth development centres.

An important part of the youth programme's work is simply exchanging information. In this way youth workers in all the Commonwealth countries can be kept abreast of developments, whether they are practical, theoretical or experimental. The results of research and surveys, reports from holders of bursaries and fellowships, contacts with universities, international bodies, governments, all these can be made available. This information activity has succeeded in bringing to a wider audience details of new and potentially valuable methods of dealing with universal problems. In Botswana, for instance, an imaginative use has been made of radio in involving the people in national planning, and young people played an important part in the project.

In 1973 the government of Botswana ran a teaching programme in connection with its five-year development plan. It used a technique in which radio programmes on the subject were broadcast to organised groups of between five and 20 people. Each group had a trained leader from the local community, and at the end of each programme he filled in a report form and questionnaire and returned it to the organisers. All the youth groups in Botswana took part in some way, such as through youth radio learning groups. In this way the young people of Botswana were able to join their elders in learning about and commenting on the government's plans — a remarkable achievement in participation.

Many Commonwealth countries have programmes of national service for their young people — either voluntary or compulsory — and in 1975 the Commonwealth Youth Programme organised a workshop on the subject in Accra, Ghana. It was attended by directors of national youth programmes from ten African countries, as well as by representatives from India, Jamaica and Malaysia. Although these countries had various forms of national youth service programmes, their approach was somewhat different. In Malaysia, for instance, it was seen as a voluntary effort with the emphasis on providing help in emergencies, such as floods. In Nigeria, with a military government, it was compulsory for students to serve a year in the National Youth Service Corps after graduating, and its objects were a good deal sterner — to inculcate discipline, raise the moral tone and "develop in our youth attitudes of mind, acquired through shared experience and suitable training, which will make them more amenable to mobilisation in the national interest".

The Commonwealth Youth Programme is particularly concerned

with the problems involved in unemployment among young people. A paper which it published in 1975 discussed this problem, and, although it referred in particular to Africa, its conclusions have a wider application. They show that youth programmes are part of a wider pattern and cannot be isolated from such issues as rural development, as this short extract makes clear:

"Because youth form 80 per cent of the rural to urban migrants and the majority of the urban unemployed, a critical strategy of youth programmes will continue to be attempts to alleviate and perhaps eliminate rural to urban drift of school leavers. This implies that youth planners will need to study and hold dialogue with educators, youth and rural development planners to identify the extent to which their programmes can be made complementary to one another, mutually reinforcing and goal specific."

The Commonwealth Youth Programme is a major effort by governments, to foster social development in member countries. Other programmes for young people are carried out by a large number of voluntary organisations on a far smaller scale and with more limited aims.

A youth project which began in Britain and spread to the rest of the Commonwealth is the Duke of Edinburgh's award. The Duke of Edinburgh launched it in 1956 with a call to young people to make the best use of their leisure in discovering their own talents and serving their community. It wasn't intended to apply overseas at that time; it was a purely British operation. But it now operates in more than 40 Commonwealth territories, including dependencies. Sometimes it goes under a different name. For instance, when it began in Kenya in 1966 it was merged with a new President's award.

The age limits are 14 to 21 — or in some countries 24 — and there are three classes — bronze, silver and gold. But, although these sound like the medals in the Olympic Games, the Duke of Edinburgh's awards are not competitive. To win them boys and girls have to pass tests in various subjects, such as service to the community and physical fitness.

Thousands of young people from all over the Commonwealth have already responded to the challenge of these awards. Periodic expeditions are organised to bring together gold award holders from the countries in which the scheme operates.

Another kind of expedition, which owes its existence to the vision of one man, is COMEX — the Commonwealth Expedition. This was started in 1965 by Lt. Col. Lionel Gregory, with over two hundred students from British universities travelling overland to India. Since then there has been a series of similar expeditions drawing in people from many other Commonwealth countries, but all with the same intention — "to set aside the barriers of colour, class, creed and wealth, to demonstrate the Commonwealth spirit, as others have done before and during the Second World War, to arouse a new awareness in the Commonwealth and to use it as a starting point in better world relations".

The words are those of Col. Gregory himself; when he began he received no encouragement from the British government — rather the opposite. However, the Duke of Edinburgh was to comment later: "There were any number of people who thought that Comex 1 couldn't succeed. People thought it was crazy; that there was too much risk; it simply couldn't be done. But it was done, and it was a success."

Back to Col. Gregory: "Comex is not concerned with the question of training leaders or followers. All play their parts, at times as leaders, at others as followers. The central philosophy is to draw on the talents and abilities of everyone, to accept their strengths and weaknesses and rely on individuals bringing out the best in each other while appreciating the limitations of ordinary men and women. Where there is kindness, to express gratitude; where there is squalor, to produce cleanliness; where there is misery, to generate hope; where there is no hygiene, to introduce it; where there is sadness, to create happiness; where there is loneliness, to offer friendship; where there is poverty, to show compassion; where there is confusion, to produce order; where there is hysteria, to display calm; where there is arrogance, to be humble; where there is ignorance, to show understanding. These became the Everests of Comex. For it was never the purpose of these expeditions to build schools or bridges or roads, but to produce a little friendship — and that takes a lot of doing."[1]

The Boy Scout and Girl Guide movements are well established in many countries and have always shown a particular interest in the

(1) From an article on Comex 7 in "Commonwealth" Feb/Mar 1975.

Commonwealth. The Scout Association has a Commonwealth department at its headquarters, for instance, and one of the badges which girl guides can win requires an above average knowledge of the Commonwealth

Less well-known, and a good deal younger, is the Commonwealth Youth Exchange Council, formed in 1970 to foster contacts between young people from Britain and other Commonwealth countries. Membership is open to any British-based organisation which has an interest in exchanges of this sort, with associate membership open to equivalent organisations in the other member countries.

The Council provides information and advice and promotes funding for youth exchanges, which are broadly "interpreted to include group visits which will hopefully lead to reciprocal exchanges and projects such as school linking, which encourage contact between young people of Britain and other Commonwealth countries".

There are certain conditions. The programme must be a purposeful one and should involve direct contact with young people from the host country and, wherever possible, stays in private homes, the visit must be sponsored by a reputable organisation and led by a responsible person, most members of the group must be between the ages of 15 and 30, and the visit should last for anything from 10 days to 10 months. Among the exchanges which have taken place under the auspices of the CYEC: Kenyan young farmers and Indian graduates have visited Britain, a London school cricket team went to Jamaica, and a Jamaican cadet band went to Britain.

Another little-known scheme promoting visits by young (or at least, youngish) people is what is known rather long-windedly as Commonwealth Interchange Study Group Operation, or CISGO. Like the Commonwealth Youth Exchange Council, this is concerned at present with visits to or from Britain, although the intention is eventually to organise visits between other Commonwealth countries.

CISGO was started in 1966 by the Royal Commonwealth Society (see Chapter Ten) in order to fill a gap in the international travel scene. It is for promising young men and women in business or the professions who have little or no opportunities for learning about other countries through personal contact. The age limits are 25 to 35, those taking part are nominated by their employers or professional associations, and they travel in groups numbering usually between 15 and 20 and representing as many different backgrounds as possible. Their visits last for three or four weeks, and where possible they stay in private homes.

Up to the end of 1975 ten CISGO trips had been held, some from Britain to other Commonwealth countries, some the other way. One was neither. Shortly before Britain became a member of the European Community a group from eleven Commonwealth countries, including Britain, visited what were then the six member nations of the Community.

Probably the best-known activity of all is the Commonwealth Games, which like the Olympic Games, are held every four years. Indeed, they rank only second to the Olympics as an international sporting event. The games in New Zealand in 1974 brought together some 1500 young athletes from all over the Commonwealth.

The idea of holding the games is an old one; it was first suggested in a letter to the London *Times* as long ago as 1891. But it wasn't until 1930 that the first Empire Games were held in Canada, largely through the initiative of the Canadian team manager at the Olympics in Amsterdam two years earlier. Since 1930 they have been held regularly, apart from a period during and immediately after the war. They have almost always been in white Commonwealth countries, the single exception being 1966, when they were in Jamaica. But this is likely to change, just as the use of the word British has been dropped from the title (rather belatedly) as the games have acknowledged the reality of the contemporary Commonwealth.

The Commonwealth fortunately doesn't possess countries which deliberately train athletes to prove the superiority of their social system, and the games are considerably less nationalistic in tone than the Olympics. They have been described (rather optimistically, perhaps) as setting international rivalry within family fellowship.

What with exchange visits, expeditions, awards and other efforts to capture the imagination of young people, it is clear that there is a great deal of Commonwealth-wide activity — although perhaps little enough in relation to the numbers of people involved. But what about the voice of the young themselves? How do they view what we insist on looking on as a problem? Here are a few extracts from an essay written by a 14-year-old girl who won a competition organised by the Royal Commonwealth Society. The theme was whether young people in different countries, particularly in the Commonwealth, had more in common with each other than with their elders in their own countries. On the whole she seemed to think they did:

"Perhaps the youth of the world today adopts new standards, which it accepts as normal, because it has lost faith in the ability of the older generation to make this world a better place to live in.

"Youth today is continually exposed to the threat of war, pollution and starvation, all of which it rejects as unnecessary and undesirable. The older generations seem to accept these horrors as inevitable, and so the youth of today protests against the "Establishment" by rejecting the standards of the older generation within its own society.

"Youth must play its part in bridging the generation gap, particularly in the Commonwealth, and look for new ways of establishing common interests with the older generation within its own society. To protest against the "Establishment" and to adopt different standards to the older generation causes friction between the different age groups and is just as negative as the older generation saying that the youth of today has lost its values."

CHAPTER SIX

Willingly To School

There was a time — and it wasn't all that long ago — when education in the Commonwealth was centred on Britain. Children in African villages or palm-fringed islands in the Caribbean and the Pacific would solemnly write about the battle of Agincourt or learn passages of Shakespeare, remote from their own experience. Their knowledge of other Commonwealth countries was gained through British eyes — India was the story of the East India Company, not of the Indian people, Africa of Livingstone and Rhodes. This is changing, and the modern Commonwealth is helping to change it.

Commonwealth co-operation in education has a long history. The first imperial education conference was held in 1912. There were others — in 1923 and 1927 — then no more until well after the war. The year 1913 saw the foundation of the Association of Commonwealth Universities, with a membership of about 50 institutions. The past 30 years have seen an enormous expansion of university education in the developing countries, and membership is now over 200.

The association promotes the movement of staff between Commonwealth universities by helping member institutions to fill vacant posts, by travel grants for senior administrators and academic exchanges. It publishes a Commonwealth Universities Yearbook and guides to awards. It also plays a large part in the Commonwealth Scholarship and Fellowship Plan. This was the result of the first post-war education conference of the Commonwealth, held at Oxford in 1959. At this conference it was acknowledged that: "The free association in the Commonwealth of countries which share a belief in the common principles of justice, a democratic way of life and personal freedom affords a special opportunity for the pooling of resources.

There is an obligation on those with more highly developed educational facilities to help their fellow-members. But all races and peoples have made their characteristic contribution to the building of knowledge, culture and values, and all have something to give."

In 1959 many of the present members of the Commonwealth were still British dependencies, and there have been enormous political changes since then in other ways. Nevertheless, the scholarship and fellowship plan has flourished. More than a thousand scholarships are held in any one year, and they are by no means entirely in the developed countries. They are mostly for postgraduate study, a source of some complaint from some of the smaller countries who have few students sufficiently qualified to take advantage of them.

Take, for instance, this sad comment from the Atlantic island colony of St. Helena in the report on the scheme for the academic year 1974/75: "St. Helena . . . has not been able to make very great use of the plan, as few of our secondary pupils have as yet gained the required O and A levels and are therefore not eligible for even the undergraduate scholarships."

However, most Commonwealth countries seem well satisfied with the operation of the scheme. The number of them who provide scholarships has grown over the years and includes the developed nations, African countries (Nigeria, Ghana and Sierra Leone), Malta and Cyprus, Jamaica and several countries in Asia. This gives Commonwealth scholars a great variety of possible courses. In 1974/75, for example, a Nigerian was studying veterinary science in Australia, an Indian English in Britain, a Briton Buddhism in India, a Ugandan inorganic chemistry in Hong Kong and a Canadian zoology in Nigeria.

Five Commonwealth countries — Australia, Britain, Canada, India and New Zealand — have instituted Fellowships of varying duration for senior academics. There are separate categories of Senior Medical Fellows, Medical Fellows and Commonwealth Academic Staff Fellows awarded at British universities.

Commonwealth education conferences are now held regularly every three years at ministerial level, and the emphasis of their discussions has changed in accordance with the changed needs of the member countries. From the 1974 conference, held in Kingston, Jamaica, came a suggestion for a Commonwealth programme for applied studies in education. It was proposed by the then Secretary-General, Mr. Arnold Smith, who thought the programme could bring together "educationists, sociologists, economists and administrators to undertake on an interdisciplinary basis research into fundamental problems facing ministries of education throughout the Commonwealth".

A study group drawn from various member countries was set up to consider this proposal; it made a number of recommendations to be considered at the 1977 conference in Accra. What these amounted to in essence was the establishment of a "practical and problem solving enterprise" at the service of member governments and with the Secretariat as its focal point.

The study group identified some of the problems which such an enterprise — bringing together practitioners of different disciplines — might be called on to solve — for example, universal primary education and "drop outs" from the school system. It considered that the problem of universal primary education was likely to loom so large that it devoted a section of its report to describing it. Here is its account of the background:

"It is now possible to see the deficiencies of policies that set out to achieve universal primary education by using the traditional "school model" as the instrument of policy. The cost in terms of plant, equipment and teachers is such that many countries have had to lengthen their timetables for its achievement. The policy has, moreover, produced side effects which have presented new and difficult problems for governments to grapple with; for example, how to provide literacy programmes for pupils who have dropped out of school; what to do with young people who have succeeded in their education in terms of the criteria of success of the school system but who have been unable to find employment and who have become "unemployed intellectuals"; the loss of talent from rural communities; and the development of false expectations in the minds of people who then find technical and other forms of vocational training beneath them.

"There has been a loss of confidence in traditional models of schools and teacher education institutions and much anxious searching for new models of education that will enable governments to achieve the objectives of universal primary education in ways that are consistent with their national plans for development. Projects are underway in a number of countries, including Commonwealth countries."

Co-operation in education at the official level comes from the Commonwealth Education Liaison Committee, on which all governments are represented. This is an advisory and consultative body, working with the education division of the Commonwealth Secretariat. The division itself, which has nine professional members, is concentrating on a few selected areas of activity, with the aim of helping the developing countries to set up educational systems with limited resources. One is what is called curriculum renewal — that is, enabling them to teach their children along lines more relevant to their lives. This takes time, and they need help to establish curriculum renewal projects and centres and to train people.

The division launched a Commonwealth Book Programme in 1972. This exists to consider problems faced in the local production of textbooks and other teaching materials and to make available copyright-free material for reproduction and translation. The division is also concerned with teacher training and scientific and technical education and through regular publications acts as a clearing house for information on selected areas of education.

One of its main priorities is what is known as non-formal approaches to education. What this means is mass education through correspondence, radio or television — methods by which countries with little money to spare and few teachers can take education to every village.

A spectacular example of this was the mass experiment carried out in India for a year from July 1975 and known as SITE (Satellite Instructional Television Experiment). By the use of an American satellite 2400 Indian villages were enabled to receive special television programmes for four hours each day. Special sets — and in many cases a supply of electricity — were provided to the selected villages for communal viewing. The programmes were aimed at three distinct audiences — adults, schoolchildren and teachers. The last two groups were included because of the enormous wastage rate of children from primary schools in India — as high as 60 per cent. It was hoped that television instruction would make school more attractive and interesting.

There were inevitably technical troubles. The experiment began during the monsoon season; high winds damaged receiving aerials, and floods made access to some of the villages impossible for the repair teams, except by boat. But, although the results of the experiment were still being evaluated months after it ended, the indications were that the audiences enjoyed the programmes, learned a good deal from them and wanted them to continue.

Obviously the spread of education through satellite television could be applied in many other countries, and in April 1976 the Commonwealth Secretariat and the Commonwealth Broadcasting Association (see Chapter Ten) jointly organised a study visit to SITE for a group of people from 13 Commonwealth countries; they represented both the educational and broadcasting professions. They were impressed by what they saw, not least by the fact that, apart from the satellite itself, all the technology was of Indian manufacture.

Radio offers a more flexible and cheaper tool for the teacher, although one with less impact. In October 1975 educators and radio and television broadcasters came together for the first Commonwealth Educational Broadcasting conference in Sydney. The Australian Education Minister, Mr. Kim Beazley, summed up the potential advantages of using the mass-media:

"In many countries teachers with even moderate qualifications are few in number; specialist teachers — in science and technology, languages, mathematics, management or the education of the handicapped, for example — are fewer still. Broadcasting, both radio and television, can be invaluable in supplementing scarce human resources."

The conference made a number of recommendations stressing the importance of educational broadcasting. Its greatest achievements, according to a Nigerian delegate, were "the creation of a forum for educationists and broadcasters to discuss their peculiar problems, thereby enabling them to appreciate one another's point of view", the sharing of experience and the establishment of personal links.

An important aspect of education is its administration. In 1971 a Commonwealth Council for Educational Administration was established with headquarters at the University of New England in New

South Wales, Australia. The case for its existence was stated in its first newsletter:

"In most countries of the Commonwealth expenditure upon education accounts for a very large proportion of national resources. Yet the people chosen to administer these expensive educational enterprises have often been ill-prepared and, in the professional sense of practice in the field of administration, ill-supported by the necessary human contacts with colleagues of similar interests, by the supply of journals in the area or by opportunities to discuss matters of mutual concern in conferences, meetings and the like."

It needs to be added that the Commonwealth Secretariat conducted a series of three regional workshops aimed at providing on-the-spot training for educational administrators. A first substantive training course for the African region was planned for early 1977.

CHAPTER SEVEN

Legal And Medical

When Britain colonised other parts of the world it introduced its own concept of law. But this doesn't mean that there is one legal system throughout the Commonwealth. In each country English law existed side by side with local law — or in some cases the law introduced by earlier colonisers — so that now there is a great patchwork of legal systems in the Commonwealth.

To take a single instance: in India the English found Hindu and Moslem laws in force. They gradually made local regulations to suit local conditions. They established a uniform criminal law, including independent magistrates hearing evidence extracted by cross- examination in court. They developed laws on the English model to deal with contract and companies, factories and worker compensation. But they left alone a great deal of existing legislation, on religious matters for instance, and on personal and family affairs, such as marriage, adoption, inheritance and succession.

A similar pattern is seen elsewhere. In Sri Lanka, which in the past was governed by the Portuguese and the Dutch as well as the British, there are still four different forms of law. In Mauritius and Seychelles, which were once French possessions, French law still operates in certain areas. Many African countries have their own tribal customary law.

The result is that independent Commonwealth countries have inherited a varied legal framework on which they are now building in accordance with their needs — laws, after all, are a necessary part of economic and social development. But English law has had a profound effect on this framework. The English method is one of building up law from precedents in individual cases and individual statutes, not laying down a rigid code. The concept of "common law" goes hand in hand with various techniques, such as trial by jury, and also with the idea of the rule of law – the belief that the individual has certain rights which even the state cannot usurp, and that he should obtain justice in the courts "without distinction of race, religion, wealth, social status or political influence".

It was lawyers themselves, not their governments, who initiated their own form of Commonwealth co-operation. The first conference of Commonwealth lawyers was held in London in 1955 and attended by 600 people. They discussed law reform, the training of future lawyers and the problems of legal aid. In 1960 there was another meeting, in Ottawa, and in 1965 about 3000 delegates attended a law conference in Sydney.

Although these conferences have continued, governments have now taken a hand. In 1966 there was a meeting of law ministers and attorneys general in London, mainly to discuss changes in the law relating to fugitive offenders in Commonwealth countries. It followed the case of Chief Anthony Enaharo, whom the British government had extradited to Nigeria; under the law as it stood, the government said, it had no choice. But the charges against Chief Enaharo were politically inspired, and the object of the meeting was to amend the law so that in future fugitive offenders could not be returned to face political charges.

Meetings of law ministers are now held regularly and are organised by the legal division of the Secretariat. They take place in different countries; they are concerned with matters of practical co-operation. For instance, the agenda of a meeting in Lagos in 1975 included such items as the reciprocal enforcement of judgements, arbitral awards and maintenance orders; extradition, following up bankruptcy assets abroad, harmonising patent and trade mark laws and an exchange of ideas on a wide range of topics, such as bail, legal aid, developments in penology, and privacy and the law.

One result of the ministerial meetings was the introduction in 1974 of the Commonwealth Law Bulletin, designed to keep member countries informed of significant developments in the legal field. The bulletin is issued quarterly by the legal division and gives brief details of new legislation, important judicial decisions, international agreements and measures of law reform in member countries. Anyone interested can then apply direct to the country concerned for more information. For instance, one issue of the bulletin noted that the Australian government was examining the operation of the breathalyser law for drunken drivers, together with the recommendations of the law reform commission. Drunken drivers are a problem for most governments, and clearly the information gathered in Australia could be usefully applied in other countries. The bulletin now goes to governments, Members of Parliament, libraries, universities, law faculties and members of the profession in more than 46 countries.

The legal division of the Secretariat also handles a large number of requests from Commonwealth governments for information. Some examples are: an enquiry from Barbados for details of Commonwealth legislation requiring Members of Parliament and holders of public office to disclose their assets; from Cyprus on legislation on the conservation of the foreshore and river beds; from Guernsey on legislation on insurance companies; from St. Kitts on the extent to which juries are employed in criminal cases in the Commonwealth; and from Uganda on Commonwealth practice relating to the appointment of senior counsel.

Often the need is for more than information, and in co-operation with the Commonwealth Fund for Technical Co-operation the division sends legal experts on such varied topics as taxation, mineral exploitation, constitution-making and law reform. It assists in finding judges and magistrates when they are wanted, too.

A vital aspect of its work is in training legislative draftsmen. The meeting of law ministers in London in 1973 noted that there was a widespread shortage of draftsmen and recommended that early steps should be taken to overcome it. The shortage has been a serious handicap to many countries, because framing the necessary laws is a key factor in development. A survey carried out by consultants appointed by the Secretariat in 1973 showed that member countries would need between 120 and 150 draftsmen over the next three years.

A training programme was begun on a regional basis in the Caribbean, West Africa, East Africa and Asia. By early 1977 the governments of Jamaica, Barbados, Trinidad, Ghana, Nigeria, Kenya, Sri Lanka and India had acted as hosts. The courses provided basic instruction, followed by practical experience of legislative drafting under supervision. This training will remain necessary for some time to come, and its importance is shown by the opening sentences of a manual on legislative drafting prepared by the Secretariat:

"Once a person's interest has been aroused in this particular branch of the law, he will quickly appreciate its vital importance in the orderly method of government. The scope of the legal problems which will come the way of a draftsman is almost unlimited, and he will experience the fascination of the use of words and the correct choice of words for the solution of any particular problem. His work as a draftsman must be related to the practical goal of preparing laws which can be readily understood and which will carry out the policies of the government in a form acceptable to Parliament.

"A meticulous attention to detail and a clear systematic approach to any problem are vital. An analytical mind is also essential to good drafting. A draftsman must keep himself informed of events in his own country and in the world generally. He should be in a position to appreciate the political, economic and social policies that will undoubtedly be the background to the legislation he drafts."

A feature of Commonwealth co-operation in legal matters has been a possibility of overlap between some of the functions of the Secretariat and that of another body called the Commonwealth Legal Advisory Service. This was set up by the British Institute of International and Comparative Law in 1962. Like the legal division of the Secretariat, which came into being seven years later, it has provided (but not funded) experts and information needed by member governments. It was originally financed by the British Institute, then by the British government, then by a number of Commonwealth governments.

It has now reached an understanding with the Secretariat's legal division under which, in an attempt to avoid duplication, senior officers of both bodies meet regularly to discuss projects.

There are several other bodies engaged in particular aspects of co-operation in legal matters. The Commonwealth Legal Education Association was established in 1971 as a result of discussions at a Commonwealth law conference in New Delhi. There have been many innovations in the teaching of law; it is an era of change, and it is important for knowledge and ideas to be shared. The objects of the association are to promote legal education and research through contacts, exchanges and collaboration generally.

Another body, the Commonwealth Legal Bureau, has as one of its priorities the encouragement of strong, viable organisations of lawyers in countries where none exist — mostly the developing countries. It was formed in 1969 and has held annual meetings in different parts of the Commonwealth.

Finally, there is the Commonwealth Magistrates Association, whose aims include promoting the interests of the office of magistrate and safeguarding its independence, disseminating information and encouraging liaison. The association dates from 1970. Its conferences have discussed such problems as the treatment of offenders, the organisation and procedure of the court, legal education and the training of the judiciary and court staff. An interesting experiment was carried out at its conference in Nairobi in 1973. Delegates from each country took part in an exercise which enabled them to compare the sentences they would impose for the same offence.

Legal co-operation between Commonwealth countries seems bound to intensify as increasingly they seek their own patterns of development from a common base. In the words of Mr. Lee Kuan Yew, Prime Minister of Singapore: "We inherited basic institutions and concepts of government and society. We understand each other better than any other group do. We use the same diction and concepts. It does not mean that we all stay put. We are all evolving and discovering our own personalities."

There is a rather similar picture in the fields of medicine and health. Many Commonwealth countries have broadly similar systems for providing health services, and Commonwealth universities and medical schools often exchange teachers and students. So it is natural for Commonwealth countries to co-operate, and they do so in a number of ways.

Health ministers usually head their country's delegations to the Commonwealth medical conferences, which began in 1965. Their discussions are severely practical, as was shown by the list of topics covered at their meeting in Colombo in 1974. The general theme was how to choose from different goals, when the needs are unlimited and the resources are scarce, and the conference focussed on several different areas.

As we have seen, the emphasis in economic development is now on rural regions so as to increase food production and stop the drift to the cities. The Colombo conference tackled the problem of how to build up health services in the rural areas when in most countries the hospitals and the doctors are in the cities. Many developing countries are establishing a network of rural health centres, which can have mobile units attached to them for outlying villages, and are linked to hospitals in district regional centres, to which more complex cases can be sent.

The idea is that these centres would be manned by medical auxiliaries led by fully qualified doctors. But there is a difficulty here. Doctors in rural areas feel isolated, both personally and professionally, and lack opportunities for promotion — which is why huge numbers of people in these areas are without adequate medical care. The conference went into this in some detail and recommended various incentives for doctors to work in the countryside. The main inducement, it was felt, would be to create conditions which gave doctors some satisfaction in their jobs, allied perhaps to special allowances and subsidies for housing and travel.

The Colombo conference also discussed a completely different problem — the health hazards in towns and cities caused by pollution, industrialisation and mechanisation. It emphasised the need for such measures as providing homes with piped water and proper waste disposal and building low-cost housing to counteract the spread of shanty towns. It looked, too, at the question of family planning, the "brain drain" of doctors, the difficulty of maintaining expensive medical equipment in repair and the possibility of bulk purchase of drugs. In most cases the conference recommended action.

This underlines the fact that these conferences are not simply talking shops; they do lead to positive action. A small but typical example comes from the discussions held by Commonwealth representatives — mostly senior medical officers — when they met in Geneva in April 1976 before the assembly of the World Health Organisation. The representative from Mauritius told the meeting that his government had now begun to send senior specialists and consultants to rural areas, as recommended by the Commonwealth medical conference. The object, he said, was to bring medicine to the people, rather than the people to medicine.

At the same meeting another innovation was mentioned. The Malaysian representative said that a flying doctor service, using helicopters, was being developed in his country, and the response from the public was encouraging. Here is an idea which was pioneered in a Commonwealth country — Australia — as long ago as 1928. The idea is simple enough. To cover large rural areas why not a doctor flying in a light plane bringing relief — and perhaps life — to sick people who might otherwise have to travel for days to receive attention? From Australia the idea spread in the nineteen-fifties and sixties to Commonwealth countries in Africa. So much interest was aroused by publicity about the flying doctor services that they were later introduced in countries outside the Commonwealth. The Malaysian experience shows that the idea is still spreading.

Medical co-operation between Commonwealth countries in the same region has been actively promoted, to ensure that scarce and expensive facilities are used to the fullest extent possible. The first to go in for this form or regional collaboration, in 1969, were Caribbean health ministers. There is contact with the Commonwealth as a whole through the Secretariat's medical adviser, and the Secretariat helps with regional health projects — a regional survey on dental health and planning the curriculum for nursing education were among them.

There are two regional health secretariats in Africa which were established with support from the Commonwealth Secretariat. One, which dates from 1972, is in Lagos and was formed by the four Commonwealth countries in West Africa — Nigeria, Ghana, Sierra Leone and The Gambia. A fifth state, Liberia, which is English-speaking although outside the Commonwealth, joined later. The secretariat's activities have so far centred on post-graduate medical education; the training of health personnel, including training in management for senior doctors, and in hospital maintenance; and the exchange of information on communicable diseases. A West African post-graduate medical college was established in 1973.

A similar health secretariat was set up in 1974 in Arusha, Tanzania, to cover Commonwealth countries in East, Central and Southern Africa. Here the emphasis has been on the training of teachers for medical auxiliaries, developing textbooks and manuals for them, and arrangements for visiting specialists to give short courses to doctors already in practice.

Both these African centres have become involved in health management training — enabling countries to cope with the organisational changes needed to develop their health services in the remoter and needier areas. The Commonwealth Secretariat has helped with advice, technical expertise and finance.

The work of the Secretariat's medical section is likely to expand in the direction of supporting training schemes. For example, the Nigerian government had a large-scale plan to develop health services in the rural areas. It was short of trained staff, and it turned to the Commonwealth Secretariat, among others, to recruit the people to do the training. Nigeria, being a major oil producer, can pay for their services; other countries less able to pay can be helped by the Commonwealth Fund for Technical Co-operation.

There is a great deal of unofficial Commonwealth co-operation in medical matters, some of it is of long standing. The Commonwealth Medical Advisory Bureau is maintained by the British Medical Association to welcome doctors visiting Britain from other parts of the Commonwealth and give them advice and help during their stay. The Commonwealth Medical Association, which shares the same headquarters, is an association of doctors. Its aim is to promote the interests of medical science and maintain the honour and traditions of the profession. It awards travelling fellowships to enable distinguished physicians or teachers, or both, to visit member associations. There are also Commonwealth-wide associations of nurses and pharamacists, both of which are concerned with furthering the interests of these professions and helping with the formation of national associations.

Commonwealth co-operation in science is maintained by unofficial and personal links, as well as more formally through the Commonwealth Science Council. This is a body whose antecedents derive from the 1930s. As now constituted it is an inter-governmental organisation whose object is the fullest possible collaboration between member countries in increasing their capacity to use science and technology for economic and social development. It meets every two years in a different Commonwealth country and has recently adopted a far more active role than before.

The Council has been concentrating on such aspects of development as infrastructure in rural communities, non-conventional energy resources, preserving and storing food, pollution, standards for engineering and industrial products, industrial research and training, scientific management, and geological surveys and mineral exploitation. One particular problem it has worked on is how to communicate the findings of research to potential users. A workshop on communications techniques was held for African countries at Arusha in April 1976. At its meeting at the end of 1976, the Council agreed on an expanded programme of collaborative research into projects reflecting the needs of member countries.

There is a large number of Commonwealth bodies concerned with particular aspects of science. The Commonwealth Committee on Mineral Resources and Geology, formed in 1948, promotes co-operation between official organisations concerned with these subjects. The Commonwealth Collection of Micro-organisms encourages the expansion of culture collections and their wider use in the Commonwealth.

No less than 13 bureaux and institutes deal with specialised fields of agricultural science and act as clearing houses for information. One is in Trinidad — the Commonwealth Institute of Biological Control. The others are in Britain: the Commonwealth Institutes of Entomology and Helminthology and the Commonwealth Mycological Institute; the Commonwealth Bureaux of Agricultural Economics, Animal Breeding and Genetics, Animal Nutrition, Dairy Science and Technology, Horticulture and Plantation Crops, Pastures and Field Crops, Plant Breeding and Genetics, Soils and the Commonwealth Forestry Bureau.

The expanded programme of the Commonwealth Science Council seems likely to be the first sign of a change in the pattern of scientific collaboration, with a greater emphasis on alternative technology. In a speech to Commonwealth Parliamentarians in 1976 the Secretary-General, Mr. Ramphal, had this to say: "I must confess that the Commonwealth scientific effort seems to me to have been wholly inadequate to the needs and opportunities of the situation. Given the Commonwealth's greatly increased involvement with the problems of poverty and development, the time is opportune to remedy this deficiency. Far too much of the thrust of research and development efforts has hitherto been concentrated on the comparatively sophisticated technological needs of industry. A more basic, low-cost but no less innovative programme at the neglected grass roots level could yield immeasurable benefits to vastly greater numbers of people. The Secretariat can make a real contribution to the development effort by promoting effective Commonwealth collaboration in these fields."

CHAPTER EIGHT

A Family Of Parliaments

One of the most important links between Commonwealth countries is the tradition of Parliamentary democracy. From the earliest days British colonies of settlement had legislative assemblies. And in this century one of the features of newly independent Commonwealth countries was their Parliaments, fashioned on the Westminster model.

Many of these countries have modified this model to suit their own conditions; others have abandoned it to become military regimes, with Parliament at least temporarily in abeyance. All the same, the Commonwealth Parliamentary Association has more than 90 branches; Parliamentary democracy is more vigorous in the Commonwealth than many people imagine.

The CPA began life in 1911 as an Empire Parliamentary Association, confined to the dominions and run by the United Kingdom. Its first inspiration came from the then Colonial Secretary, Mr L. S. Amery, who asked: "Why should not the Coronation (of George V) be made the occasion for calling together representatives of all free Parliaments of the Empire?" This suggestion was eagerly taken up and expanded by a barrister called Howard d'Egville, who had a vision of something far greater and more permanent: "An association to be called under some such title as Empire Parliamentary Union, having branches in the United Kingdom Parliament and the Parliaments of the overseas dominions, so that mutual intercourse and exchange of information should be facilitated between home and overseas members, introductions, Parliamentary privileges, travel facilities, meetings and information provided for members in the respective countries." Apart from a small change in the title, this is substantially what he got, and for many years he was its guiding light and inspiration. It was not until 1960, when he was 81, that he reluctantly retired.

He seems to have been a man of contradictions. This is how Mr. Patrick (now Lord) Gordon Walker, a former Commonwealth Secretary, described him: "d'Egville was an enigmatic, contentious, rather crabbed man who inspired admirers and detractors with equal intensity of feeling. He had, however, a vision of the Empire evolving into the Commonwealth and a deep faith in the importance of the EPA and then the CPA is sustaining and strengthening the Commonwealth. He devoted himself single-mindedly to serving this development, and he was, in fact, an idealist. . . . It is easy, however, to lose sight both of his idealism and his dedication because he was quite unscrupulous in his methods."

He had a habit of concealing unwelcome facts. Among these, as time went on, was his age, which he went to enormous lengths to keep secret, even to the extent of erasing the date of birth from his passport.

During the first 30 years or so of the life of the association, d'Egville — who was knighted in 1921 — ran it from his position as secretary of the United Kingdom branch. But the first conferences were held outside Britain — in South Africa in 1924, Australia in 1926 and Canada in 1928. He spent most of the second world war in Canada — for which he was criticised in Britain — and this fact, together with his experience of other Commonwealth countries, made him sympathetic to the idea of Commonwealth, as opposed to Empire.

It was largely through his advocacy that in 1948 the association changed its name to become the Commonwealth Parliamentary Association and instituted a central secretariat and general council, instead of being controlled by the United Kingdom branch. As Earl Attlee, then British Prime Minister, put it: "It was a natural step . . . and really very parallel to what had happened in the development of the Commonwealth and Empire."

The years after the war saw a large increase in the number of branches. There were main branches in the independent countries, whose number grew rapidly in the sixties, state or provincial branches in such countries as India, Australia, Canada and Malaysia and affiliated or auxiliary branches in territories which were still dependencies but had representative legislatures. That is the reason there are many more branches than there are independent members of the

Commonwealth. In Europe, for instance, such ancient Parliaments as those of the Isle of Man and Jersey and Guernsey are represented, as well as Westminster.

However, growth brought its own problems. Branches were entitled to be represented on the general council, but, as their number grew, the council became too large and unwieldy. In 1967 a small executive committee was set up. Branches were grouped together into seven regions, and membership of the committee was put on a regional basis, with the addition of some of the association's officers and an independent chairman.

At its first meeting the committee endorsed an important decision taken the year before by the general council. This was to turn down applications from the clerks of the former Parliaments in Ghana and Nigeria to attend the next conference as observers. In both countries there had been military coups, and their Parliaments were no longer functioning.

After considerable debate a resolution was passed which said unequivocally that "The maintenance of Parliamentary government is essential to the existence of branches and participation in CPA activities." This remains the policy of the CPA, with the result that not all members of the Commonwealth are represented in its deliberations. At the time of writing (1976) Ghana, Nigeria and Uganda had military governments and were excluded.

The official description of the CPA as it has now evolved is: "An association of Commonwealth Parliamentarians who, irrespective of race, religion or culture, are united by community of interest, respect for the rule of law and the rights and freedoms of the individual citizen and by pursuit of the positive ideals of Parliamentary democracy. In providing the sole means of regular consultation between Commonwealth Parliamentarians, the Association aims to promote understanding and co-operation among them and also to promote the study of and respect for Parliamentary institutions throughout the Commonwealth. These objectives are pursued by means of conferences, plenary and regional, the interchange of delegations, seminars, publications, notably *The Parliamentarian,* and through the work of the Parliamentary Information and Reference Centre." Let us examine this rather more closely.

Membership is open to all members of legislatures in the Commonwealth, including those in dependent territories (members who lose or give up their seats can become associates). Since the branches are autonomous the actual practice varies; in some branches all MPs are regarded as members of the CPA, in most membership is only for those interested.

The Information and Reference Centre has been set up in the General Council Secretariat opposite the Houses of Parliament in London. Its aims are to assemble a comprehensive collection of authoritative materials on Commonwealth and other legislatures, to provide a prompt information service for members and others and to publish monographs, bibliographies and shorter book lists for people working or studying in the Parliamentary field. The first monograph was on salaries and allowances of Commonwealth Parliamentarians and gave detailed figures from 76 Parliaments, as in August, 1973. This was planned to be the beginning of a series covering a number of topics, such as the financial interests and integrity of MPs and the growth of the committee system.

The Parliamentarian is published quarterly and contains articles, book reviews and book lists on subjects of Parliamentary and constitutional interest, together with reports on the major proceedings in many Commonwealth Parliaments. For example, the issue of January 1976 included important articles on the controversy surrounding the dissolution of the Australian Parliament by the Governor-General a few months earlier and on a clash between the Parliament of Zambia and members of the country's only political party.

Speakers and presiding officers of Commonwealth Parliaments have met regularly since 1969 and have discussed such subjects as relations between legislature, executive and judiciary; the effect of opinion polls on elections; privileges and immunities of members; and problems of Parliamentary procedure. Seminars on Parliamentary practice and procedure began at Westminster in 1951 and are held every year. The original idea was to give instruction to members from dependencies or newly-independent countries, but they have developed into symposia, enabling those taking part to exchange ideas and pool experience. The past few years have seen the development of regional seminars, which began in Australia in 1972 and Canada in

1973. Most of the various regions also hold conferences of their branches to discuss matters regarded as of too localised an interest to be raised at the full plenary conferences.

It is perhaps these plenary conferences which are the major activity of the CPA in the public eye. They are held every year in a different Commonwealth country, and the convention is that the president of the association comes from the branch which is to be host to the conference and the vice-president from the host branch for the following year. The immediate past-president is an *ex officio* member of the executive council, thus ensuring a certain continuity of experience.

Members attend these conferences as Parliamentarians, not as representatives of their governments, although some may, of course, be government ministers. To counteract their all too human tendency to make long, prepared speeches, time limits are imposed, and discussions are conducted in panel or committee meetings, as well as the plenary sessions.

The range of subjects covered is wide. As an example, the agenda of the Delhi conference of 1975 included the following items: The Indian Ocean as a zone of peace; developments in South-East Asia; Africa (including Rhodesia and South Africa); Europe and the countries round the Mediterranean; the world energy crisis; building a new international economic order; social problems, such as unemployment, violence, unrest among young people and drugs; the preservation of the environment; and the Commonwealth as an instrument of social, political and economic transformation.

That should have been enough to keep them talking for two years, but they only had two weeks. And, since this is an association of Parliamentarians, not government leaders or civil servants, perhaps the most absorbing debates are those on Parliament itself. In Delhi the subject was discussed from the point of view of the internal and external threats to the authority and prestige of Parliament. At previous conferences there have been vigorous debates about the merits or demerits of the one-party state. This is the system which has been introduced in several African countries — notably Zambia and Tanzania — which retain their branches of the CPA.

Nevertheless, doubts have been expressed as to whether the system can be reconciled with Parliamentary democracy, and the London conference of 1973 saw a clash of opinion on this. A Malaysian delegate expressed himself in forthright terms: "The one-party system is nothing new. We have seen it in Nazi Germany and in Fascist Italy. We cannot deny that while those parties existed great things in a way were achieved; but were they democracy? Did anyone describe these one-party states as democracies?

"The one-party system is the very antithesis of democracy. Such a thing as a one-party democracy does not exist. When one party arrogates to itself the right to decide who are to be candidates and in effect has the right to prevent others from offering themselves as candidates and even prohibits the formation of other parties, I say that it is a gross insult to the sacred institutions of democracy to allow such a state to describe itself as a democracy."

Strong words, but the one-party state had its defenders. A member from Tanzania explained the philosophy behind it: "One-party Parliamentary democracies are democracies which subscribe to the proposition that men and countries must have the absolute power to determine their destinies. Thus, the freedom of choice through universal adult suffrage during general elections, the freedom of speech, of press and of assembly and freedom to criticise are important foundations within the one-party state. So is the concept of the supremacy of Parliament.

"The machinery for providing choice occurs under the umbrella of one single party. Elections are fought on the ability of candidates to interpret the role they can play in implementing the national will rather than seemingly serious conflicts of interest. For any political system to survive there must be some basic principles which bind society together. Within this broader framework disagreement or opposition to the application of policies can be voiced. But rarely are the principles of their society questioned, for to do so the resolution of basic contradictions in a society can be achieved only through a revolution.

"Within this broad agreement under the one-party Parliamentary democracy, as with any other, government is by consent. The knowledge that a minister or member may fail to get elected, and the power of the electorate to reject candidates for any office, provide a practical basis of the democracy we have been talking about."

The debate continues, and, by keeping one-party states within the fold, whatever reservations members may have, the CPA has ensured that it can continue.

The association has not, however, been able to avoid all the strains and tension which have been evident in Commonwealth relations from time to time. During the conference in Canberra in 1970, for instance, the Zambian delegation walked out because the Zambian flag was lying on the ground. It had been blown down in a strong wind, and the fire brigade had to be called to get it back into position.

However, the delegation was not satisfied with this explanation, and President Kaunda sent a telegram to the conference announcing that Zambia would reluctantly have to withdraw from being host to the next conference because of "recent developments in the Commonwealth association and the world scene as a whole". This was at a time when the controversy over possible British arms sales to South Africa was raging, so there was some reason for Zambia's sensitivity.

In Delhi in 1975 a group of Indian opposition MPs staged a walk out during the debate on the challenges facing Parliament, because, they claimed, their own government had prevented them from speaking. The chairman's explanation was that they had not put their names forward as intending speakers. This was a few months after the government of Mrs. Indira Gandhi had declared a state of emergency which involved, among other things, putting Opposition MPs in prison without trial. This in itself might be thought a challenge to Parliament, but it was hardly mentioned during the official proceedings — and when it was mentioned it was treated as a regrettable necessity which had been grossly distorted by the Western press. The official explanation was apparently accepted without question.

In averting its eyes from such a state of affairs, the CPA was doing no more than follow the Commonwealth practice of avoiding criticism of the internal policy of a member state (which in this case happened to be the host). There are good pragmatic reasons for such a practice; the Commonwealth could hardly have survived without it. In every country there is something to criticise. But once criticism from outside starts — perhaps based on misleading reports — mutual recriminations set in, the fabric of co-operation is torn down, and in the end everybody is worse off.

It is a strong and perfectly respectable argument, although private individuals need not be under the same inhibitions as governments. But the trouble is that it can lead to a bland acceptance of the most appalling tyrannies on the principle that to draw attention to them is rocking the boat. I was reminded of this when lecturing to a group of sixth formers. They demanded to know how a Commonwealth professing the principles contained in the declaration of 1971 could continue to accept President Amin's Uganda as a member. There are various "reasonable" answers to this, but perhaps the only honest one is that we all have double standards.

There have been from time to time suggestions for a full-scale Commonwealth Parliament, the legislative counterpart of the heads of government conferences which might evolve into a regular consultative assembly. Harold Wilson floated an idea on these lines before he was first elected to office in 1964, and it even found its way into the Labour Party manifesto for that year. However, it aroused opposition in the CPA itself.

At the 1965 conference in Wellington, New Zealand, a British delegate made the point that the association had never passed resolutions or made recommendations to governments. That was not its style; what was important was a genuine exchange of views. Some delegates from Africa, however, argued that talking was a waste of time unless it led to decisions which would be binding on governments. An Australian summed up the view which has prevailed — that the CPA should not try to come to decisions which would be binding on governments, but that it should do all it could to see that its discussions had some influence on government policies. A summary report of conferences is now sent to all Prime Ministers, noting the main views expressed, and the consensus, where it exists.

In fact, the idea of a Commonwealth Parliament seems misplaced and belongs to the past. The Commonwealth is too diverse, politically, culturally, socially and economically, to be subject to an Assembly. In Europe, with which a comparison is sometimes made, circumstances are different. There is a movement towards political integration in the EEC, with the result that its Parliamentary institutions need to be strengthened, if only to keep an eye on the executive. There is no such movement in the Commonwealth. The CPA will fulfil its role of serving Parliamentary democracy by keeping the dialogue going between countries of vastly different outlook.

The value of its deliberations was described by the Speaker of the Indian Lower House (Lok Sahba), Dr. G. D. S. Dhillon, when he spoke at the end of the 1975 conference in Delhi: "The CPA meetings have been truly in the nature of a family get-together where we freely and frankly exchange our views. From these family-like meetings of ours, I have felt, we emerge every time drawn together a little more closely. These meetings in different parts of the Commonwealth in turn have helped the members to visit different countries to see for themselves and know at first hand the lands and the people, their hopes and aspirations, their ways of living, their ways of thinking and their problems. This makes for deeper understanding of each other and better appreciation of each other's policies and positions in the domestic and international spheres and thus paves the way for active co-operation and collaboration for mutual development."

CHAPTER NINE

A Privileged Minority?

Here is a potted version of one aspect of recent Commonwealth history: "Our leaders were often men who were trained in the United Kingdom. There they imbibed the British values of tolerance, democracy, parliamentarianism and independence. They returned home determined to re-make their countries in the same image. The years since then have proved that this is a more difficult task than was first imagined. The rhetoric of independence was hollow if it was not accompanied by the benefits of economic development and social integration.

"The leaders then discovered that there was a vital need for expertise if the fundamental problems of nation building, economic progress, social transformation and national unity were to be overcome. This resulted in an awareness that there was a need to co-opt and develop expertise so that governments could function in the manner in which they should. This quest has led to an emphasis on the need for education. There has also been the co-option of the newer technocratic élite into the political and economic activities of the nation and the emergence of a second generation political leadership which, instead of chanting the rhetoric which moves mountains, possesses the specialised skills which instead creates mountains, builds bridges and houses and overcomes the draconian problems of developing societies.

"This necessitates an understanding of the specialised features of the professional in our societies. Their value to the government and their societies arises out of their importance to the modernising process."

The speaker was Mr. A Rahim Ishak, Minister of State for Foreign Affairs in the government of Singapore. The occasion was the opening of a conference on the role of the professions in a changing world in Singapore in October 1971.

Another speaker at the conference, Mr. Robert Steel, Secretary of the Commonwealth Association of Surveying and Land Economy (CASLE) contributed a few more thoughts on the same theme: "It is probably safe to assume than in every Commonwealth country there is general recognition of the need for lawyers, without whom none but the most primitive of constitutions or legal systems could be made to work; of the need for accountants to ensure efficiency and trustworthiness in business administration; and of the need for the medical, dental and pharmaceutical professions in the maintenance and improvement of health.

"With a little less confidence one assumes that the public also understands the functions of the engineer, architect, surveyor and town planner. Certainly one of the first professionals to move into any developing country is the land surveyor, for surveying and mapping are essential to the identification of natural resources and for planning and executing almost every form of development and construction project. Surveyors and lawyers are also required to authenticate land titles and to deal with a variety of land problems that lie at the heart of social, economic and even political progress. Equally, engineers, architects, surveyors and town planners make their several contributions to the construction of buildings and the quality of the built environment and to the planning and execution of national development programmes.

"In the past most developing countries relied to a large extent on expatriate professional services, but in more recent times it has become a natural ambition of every independent country to establish its own institutions and to develop its own skills."

These two quotations seen to me to sum up the case for the Commonwealth Foundation — perhaps the least understood of all the parts of this misunderstood association — which exists to foster professional links throughout the Commonwealth.

The Foundation was set up by the heads of government conference in 1965. It was a largely British initiative, inspired particularly by the writings of two Commonwealth statesmen — Lord Casey of Australia and Patrick Gordon Walker. Each had stressed the importance of the professions in strengthening the special character of the

Commonwealth and suggested the creation of some machinery through which co-operation could be increased.

The director of the Foundation, Mr. John Chadwick, said years later[1]: "It was against this background that on 1st March 1966 the Commonwealth Foundation opened its doors for business in what must have previously been the maids' bedrooms at Marlborough House. Three of us . . . had as our armoury a one page White Paper containing our terms of reference; the assurance of an annual income over the five financial years ahead; the prestige of an Australian Nobel Prizeman as our first chairman and some extremely vague conceptions of what "professional man" consisted of and where and how across the broad reaches of the Commonwealth we were to track him down. There was at that point in time neither furniture nor telephone nor money in the kitty — not even the first draft of the Trust Deed under which we must, as a charity, be registered under English law."

The Foundation has the following aims:

To encourage and support fuller representation at conferences of professional bodies within the Commonwealth;

To assist professional bodies within the Commonwealth to hold more conferences between themselves;

To facilitate the exchange of visits among professional people, especially the younger element;

To stimulate and increase the flow of professional information exchanged between the organisations concerned;

On request to assist with the setting up of national institutions or associations in countries where these do not at present exist;

To promote the growth of Commonwealth-wide associations or regional Commonwealth associations in order to reduce the present centralisation in Britain.

The Foundation was to be financed by voluntary contributions from governments; in fact, they all now contribute, and annual income in 1976 stood at about £700 000. Each country provides a trustee — usually its High Commissioner in London acting in a personal capacity, but in a few cases private individuals. The chairmen have been distinguished Commonwealth figures — Sir Macfarlane Burnet of Australia

(1) In a lecture to the Royal Society of Arts in London, May 1976.

(1966–69), Dr. Robert Gardiner of Ghana (1970–73) and Sir Hugh Springer of Barbados (1974–77).

How is the money spent? One important activity is the encouragement of Commonwealth professional co-operation. When the Foundation was formed there were a few Commonwealth professional associations already in being, covering, for example, medicine, architecture, broadcasting and forestry. The Foundation has helped them and also encouraged the establishment of many more.

The help has come in the form most welcome — grants of money. Up to £20 000 is generally offered for exploratory purposes. Then, once an association has been established with the backing of national societies, the Trustees have been willing to help over a minimum of three years with fresh grants averaging something like £10 000 a year. Associations set up as the result of backing from the Foundation include those concerned with libraries, museums, literature and language studies, veterinary science, geography, surveying and land economy, law and legal education and also magistrates, planners, pharmacists and nurses. There are some notable exceptions to the list; accountants and dentists, for instance, have not yet formed a Commonwealth association. On the other hand there are now good prospects for the creation of a Commonwealth body covering the agricultural sciences.

What benefits are conferred by these associations which could not be obtained by existing national or international bodies? One answer has been given by the Secretary of the Commonwealth Association of Architects, Mr. T. C. Colchester:[2] "The CAA has found that education is the service which member institutes put first among activities suitable for a Commonwealth organisation, and it is probably where a Commonwealth organisation stands the best chance of breaking out of the stage of merely holding conferences and up on to the level of giving a positive service to member bodies.

"Commonwealth-based professional organisations are favourably placed to work in the education field. By contrast the professional international bodies corresponding to the Commonwealth organisations (for example, the International Union of Architects as compared

(2) At the Singapore conference in 1971.

with the Commonwealth Association of Architects) are believed to have disappointingly little to their credit in the educational field. The world-based organisations have usually been in existence longer than their Commonwealth counterparts and periodically declare an objective of mutual help in professional education. Money, language, politics and wide diversities of resources and types, however, usually undermine the hopes built up."

And to quote Mr. Chadwick again: "In the first place, thanks to shared educational experiences and techniques, to inherited thought processes, standards and a general way of doing things, a group of, say, Commonwealth architects, nurses or veterinarians will be likelier at a week-long meeting to achieve practical results than they would as parties to a larger international gathering."

A number of the associations the Foundation has helped to create are still based on London, but several are in other countries, reflecting the aim of reducing centralisation in Britain. Among them are the Commonwealth Library Association (Jamaica), the Commonwealth Council of Educational Administration (New South Wales, Australia), the Association of Commonwealth Literature (Mysore, India), the Commonwealth Legal Bureau and the Commonwealth Veterinary Association (both Ontario, Canada). All the associations have helped to bring into being national professional bodies in countries where they did not exist before and have spread professional know-how and expertise vital in developing countries.

A pioneering venture of the Foundation has been the setting up of professional centres in many member countries. The object is to ensure that in countries where professional societies are new, poor and small in membership, the professions can band together and develop common services. It is an answer to mental professional isolation and a bridge between the professions themselves and between them as a body and their governments, universities and communities.

The first of these centres was set up in Uganda in 1968. In the words of Mr. Chadwick: "At the outset some fourteen for the most part new and poorly funded associations came together in Kampala and after much hard voluntary effort drew up a constitution and a scale of contributions, found suitable premises and then approached our Trustees for a launching grant. The concept was that this and later

Centres should provide shared secretarial services to all the professions willing to join in; one room offices for those who could not as yet afford such individual facilities elsewhere; conference and seminar rooms; a library and, far from least as a potential revenue earner, both bar and catering facilities.

"The idea has since caught on to a point where Centres are now in active operation in as many as nine capitals of the Commonwealth. In some cases governments have offered valuable plots of building land. In others a grant to match the Foundation's own financial contributions has been made. We can even claim the interest of one outside donor and take pride in the fact that Barclays International Development Fund, attracted by this aspect of professional co-operation, has over the past few years contributed the generous sum of £35 000 to be shared among several of the Centres whose permanent headquarters are now building."

The value of these Centres has been summed up by Mr. Robert Steel[3]: "On the basis of my observations in a number of countries and from my knowledge of what the Centres have been able to do for professions with which I am acquainted, I should like to emphasise the importance of their role in providing each profession with a base from which to operate. Among the beneficial services which a centre can provide are a secretariat which can deal promptly with correspondence and with the servicing of committees; a programme of publicity and public relations activities; a place for meetings; and a home for a library. Above all, it provides a continuity of administration that it is difficult to achieve if a profession has to rely entirely on the voluntary work and enthusiasm of its members. By these means the centre can help each profession to make maximum use of its resources in developing its own activities."

Barclays Bank is not the only outside interest to help the Foundation's activities. The Carnegie Corporation of New York has donated to a scheme to enable young civil servants from African Commonwealth countries to visit other African countries to broaden their professional experience, a scheme named after an outstanding British public servant, Sir Andrew Cohen. Guinness Overseas has provided

(3) At the Singapore meeting.

funds for medical ancillaries from Jamaica and Trinidad to attend a three-month course in Britain. There have also been donations from the Inchcape Group, National Westminster Bank and the Taylor Woodrow Charity Trust.

The Foundation also helps individual professional people to make research and study visits abroad and attend conferences and seminars which they might otherwise have to forego. Up to now, well over two thousand people have been helped by small grants. Among them are veterinary officers from some developing countries who attended a conference on beef cattle production in Edinburgh and young scientists from Asian countries who went to a regional conference of the International Geographical Union in New Zealand. The chief conditions for these grants are that the meeting should have a practical rather than a theoretical or academic aim, that those invited should have a contribution to offer and are likely to gain useful experience and that a subsidiary study tour can be arranged for successful applicants.

Study and research visits have included sending a lecturer from the University of the West Indies to Uganda and Kenya, a Nigerian-based professor of obstetrics to Papua New Guinea and a Canadian expert in adult education to East and Central Africa. Commonwealth Foundation Lectureships have enabled eminent professional people to travel to Commonwealth countries other than their own to lecture on their specialities and meet their colleagues. A comparatively new venture in the academic field is an award to establish a Chair in Modern Commonwealth Studies at the University of Leeds in Britain, to be held by a series of visiting Commonwealth scholars. The hope is that this will provide some re-thinking about the strength, weaknesses and significance of the modern Commonwealth.

The Foundation has taken a flexible view as to what constitutes a profession. Its lawyers obligingly defined it as "any vocation in which a professed knowledge of some department of learning is used in its application to the affairs of or is imparted to others." As a result, and as a matter of policy, the Trustees have increasingly directed their activities at what might be described as sub-professions.

The Foundation gave a grant for the British Institution of Fire Engineers to introduce Commonwealth scholarships in fire engineering. These have enabled fire officers to study working methods in other parts of the Commonwealth than their own or to train in Britain. A grant to the British Community Relations Commission provided bursaries in race relations for those particularly concerned with immigrants from other Commonwealth countries, such as teachers, policemen, probation officers and social workers in certain urban areas. The bursaries enable them to visit the countries the immigrants came from — normally India or the West Indies — to study their economic and social background. This scheme proved so successful that when it came to an end the Home Office in Britain took it over and continued it.

The Foundation has also helped journalists, with a contribution to the Commonwealth Press Union programme of travelling scholarships and a scheme for training financial journalists at University College, Cardiff.

It has published a reference book "Professional Organisations in the Commonwealth"[4], the second edition in 1976 giving details of no less than 1100 professional bodies. It has issued a series of "Occasional Papers" on a number of topics, ranging from a report on a regional seminar on social work training needs in East Africa to "Problems confronting the Industrial Scientist," a report of a lecture tour of India and Sri Lanka by a former technical director of the Scientific Research Council in Jamaica. It has given grants to several journals of interest to the developing countries and two of particular Commonwealth interest, "The Round Table" and "Commonwealth", the journal of the Royal Commonwealth Society.

An unusual venture — and one which is perhaps rather beyond its original terms of reference — was the construction of a training school for teachers of the deaf in Malawi. This is complete with children's dormitories, classrooms, audiological unit and homes for the trainee teachers. The intention is that it should develop into a regional Commonwealth centre for training and research. The Foundation grant also covers the cost of regular annual advisory visits by an ear, nose and throat specialist from Britain.

One criticism of which the Foundation is very conscious is that it caters for an élite. The communique after the Singapore meeting spoke of professional people in developing countries as forming "a thin

(4) Hutchinson Bentam, London £10.

upper layer of society, in many ways a privileged minority". In the first ten years of its operations the Commonwealth Foundation spent over £3½ million to help this minority carry out its work more effectively. When so many people face real poverty and hardship can expenditure of this order be justified?

This is how the question has been answered by Mr. Chadwick: "Of course there are higher short-term priorities than the improvement of a newer country's professional base. And of course the professions in the newer world do represent a privileged minority. And, again of course, some individuals will always be feathering their nests at the expense of the community.

"But as we see it in line with the terms of reference handed down to our trustees by the Commonwealth heads of government no country, rich or poor, can maintain existing standards or achieve a desired level of performance without a minimum well-trained professional and sub-professional base.

"There may well be short cuts and experiments that can be adopted in the earlier stages of development, e.g. the barefoot doctor, technician engineer, etc. But if the health of the nation, its agricultural production, communication systems, tourist and other industries are to prosper without remaining at the mercy of foreign expertise and influence, then fully qualified local teachers will be needed both for the sake of their own services and to produce the next local generation of professional and technological men and women. This means that existing antagonisms and suspicions between governments and universities on the one hand and the so-called professional élite on the other hand will have to be broken down. Thus, professionals, civil servants, politicians and academics will have to co-operate in the interests of their communities at large."

CHAPTER TEN

A Commonwealth of People

Early on a June morning in 1976 a group of blind climbers began the final ascent of the highest peak in South-East Asia — Kinabalu in Sarawak. With their sighted guides they had spent the night shivering in camp at a height of 11 000 feet. The final climb to the summit took them a matter of hours.

An observer who climbed with them commented afterwards: "There was a strong sense of achievement among the blind climbers and rightly so. To some it was like a dream, unbelievable that they had actually made it to the top, sitting 13 455 feet above the sea, higher than anyone else in South-East Asia . . .They had proved that they are great men amongst men."

This feat, undertaken by blind Malaysians, was the second such exacting mountain climb organised by the Royal Commonwealth Society for the Blind. The first was an assault on Mount Kilimanjaro in East Africa by seven blind African youths in 1969, an achievement which hit the headlines all over the world.

As one of the climbers put it as he stumbled through the rain forest at the end of his journey: "We were blind, we are now new men. We have met fear. We have conquered it. Though we still cannot see, we have walked through the gardens of the gods, and they were not angry. Soon we will be safe. It has been a fearsome and beautiful experience, has it not, my brothers?"

The expedition was not carried out as a stunt but, as the Society explained at the time, as "a demonstration to all Africa that trained blind people have the mental and physical stamina to achieve educating goals and to justify their place in the economic and social life of modern Africa . . . In the past most blind people in Africa were street

90

beggars or village dependents, living a life which was a burden to themselves and to the community. One of the purposes of this expedition is to change that image."

The Royal Commonwealth Society for the Blind dates from 1950 and, in the words of its director, Sir John Wilson — himself blind — it had many starting points and many people contributed to its foundation. In a paper presented to the Royal Society of Arts in 1971 he described the beginning of his own involvement 25 years before:

"Three of us had been sent by the British government and the Royal National Institute for the Blind to make a survey of blindness in Africa. On that day I was motoring through Tanzanian villages with an African driver when we came upon a bush dispensary with a crowd of blind people waiting beside it. There were about 40 of them, frail old men, frightened women, cringing children. The dispenser, a suave, bored African, told me that an eye specialist, flying from England to South Africa, would break his journey here to do a few operations. In the hope of cure these people had come, some walking 50 miles.

"It was one of those occasions when the fact that the Africans and I were blind made a human contact across barriers of language, distance and race. They talked about wives who had left them, land which had gone back to bush and their dead lives in those dark huts. I had read about this and imagined it, but this was my first glimpse into lives deprived altogether of possessions or of any sort of dignity and reasonable hope.

"After a while I grew impatient and asked the dispenser when the eye doctor would come. He said: 'He comes eight days from now, bwana — a week on Monday.'

"As we drove away from that grubby village and the wind blew clean through the car, I knew, with astonishment that I had not realised it before, that these were the people behind our immaculate statistics; not clean, manageable ciphers on a chart, but people with sweat-stained bodies and clumsy, defeated hands. They were inarticulate people, who would wait in their multitudes until something happened. Against them lay the force, not of apathy, but of a policy of carefully calculated priorities. That policy could be influenced only by an organisation strong enough to command attention, big enough to span a continent, simple enough to do something meaningful against the realities of an African village."

In its early days the Society's main efforts were in Africa and went into the education and rehabilitation of the blind. This work continues, but in the 1960s it expanded into the Asian Commonwealth, and the emphasis has now shifted to prevention and cure.

For instance, thousands of people have had their sight restored through operations in village eye camps in India, Bangladesh and Pakistan — the exact figure in 1975 was 76 856. Many others are operated on or treated in other ways to prevent blindness. In southern India the Society is co-operating in pioneer work to prevent child blindness caused by malnutrition. A hundred thousand children all over the world go blind each year for lack of a handful of vegetables. Eye operations are also carried out in African countries, where in conjunction with the World Health Organisation, the Society is taking part in a programme to eradicate "river blindness", carried by a variety of fly.

In its work to help people who are irrevocably blind the Society co-operates with national organisations in Commonwealth countries, many of which it founded. It provides education for blind children, training for blind workers, resettlement for blind farmers. But the problem is growing all the time. There are estimated to be four million blind people in the Commonwealth alone, mostly in the developing countries. If they marched two abreast, the column would stretch for 1100 miles. And, unless decisive action is taken, the number will double by the end of the century.

In his lecture Sir John Wilson explained that, although the Royal Commonwealth Society for the Blind plays its part with international organisations, it works through the Commonwealth for practical reasons: "We work together on a Commonwealth basis, not for any reason of political compulsion or historical nostalgia, but because for us this is the most effective way to operate. Through the Commonwealth link we have an informal, immediate contact, a means of planning and project control which, at least in our work, could not exist so readily in any other international setting."

Another body which operates on behalf of physically handicapped people is the Commonwealth Society for the Deaf, which dates from 1959. It was founded by a former Minister of State for Colonial

Affairs, the late Mr. John Dugdale, and Lady Templer, who first became involved with work for the deaf when her husband was High Commissioner to Malaysia. When she returned to Britain she and John Dugdale, who was himself partially deaf, called a meeting of organisations working for deaf people and launched the Society. Lady Templer, who is now chairman, has written of that period: "We had no funds with which to start and no achievement to our credit with which to attract support. But the other societies backed us, and we were launched as a registered charity."

Before long requests were flooding in for schools, training equipment and individual help from Commonwealth countries, many of which had no schools or other facilities for deaf people. Donations came from company funds and elsewhere. The Leverhulme Trust gave a grant for six scholarships a year, three for teachers and three for audiologists. The Wolfson Foundation gave two grants, one to establish a school for the deaf in Bombay, the other to start teacher training courses in Nigeria and Kenya. The Commonwealth Foundation's contribution to the school for teachers of the deaf in Malawi has already been mentioned. It has also provided funds to enable the Society to hold seminars for teachers of the deaf, specialist doctors and surgeons, audiologists, speech therapists and welfare workers.

The Society's most important activity is education — teaching the deaf, especially children, and teaching other people how to teach the deaf. It encourages schemes for helping adults to find jobs. It tries to arrange for children to be tested for deafness at an early age. It supports specialist schools and vocational training for deaf school-leavers. When it pioneers a small school, it hopes the government of the country concerned will take it over or support it, and this has frequently been the case. It issues a magazine for deaf children (called HI!) and operates a pen friend scheme.

But, as Lady Templer puts it: "The Commonwealth is very large, and we are very small. We have pitted our tiny resources against an enormous mass of human misfortune and unhappiness. Thanks to our many friends we have achieved results far beyond our earliest hopes and expectations. But we believe that we are only at the beginning of our usefulness. We are gaining knowledge and experience, and we now have many bases on which to build."

The societies for the blind and deaf are only two of a large number of unofficial organisations working for particular ends across national boundaries in the Commonwealth. An invaluable work of reference called "A Yearbook of the Commonwealth" lists more than 160. Some are purely bilateral (e.g. Britain–Nigeria Association); some have an interest extending well beyond the Commonwealth (e.g. Oxfam); some are very specialised (e.g. the Zebra Trust, catering for Commonwealth students in Britain) and some seem virtually moribund (e.g. Commonwealth Industries Association).

Of the remainder some date from imperial days and are adjusting with varying degrees of success to the fact of the modern Commonwealth. Others have emerged only in recent years.

Among the latter is the Commonwealth Human Ecology Council, which was formed as late as 1969, evolving from a committee on nutrition in the Commonwealth. Human ecology is described as the study of the interaction of man and human society with the environment, and the Council seeks to promote investigations which will increase awareness and understanding of the interactions. Its Secretary-General, Mrs. Zena Daysh, has written[1]: "We are primarily concerned with national human ecology case studies and the establishment of permanent ecological machinery in Commonwealth countries, and not only in Commonwealth countries. Our functions are catalytic and advisory, and we have strong relating educational and finance-raising and publications programmes."

The Council organised its first conference in Malta in 1970, and this has been followed by conferences in a number of Commonwealth capitals. It has promoted public lectures and publishes a newsletter. Increasingly it is being asked for advice by governments on planning the use of resources with due awareness of environmental issues.

The Council played a prominent part in the United Nations Habitat conference on human settlements in Vancouver in 1976. In the words of its Secretary-General, it "let the Commonwealth loose on the world" by presenting a report on the "Commonwealth Approach" and setting up a permanent link with the United Nations machinery for a human settlements programme.

(1) In a letter to the author.

The report was based on many months of study, discussion and organisation and drew on the experience of a number of Commonwealth countries. It included a description of an experimental project in India designed to create a new type of city in harmony with its natural environment. Some 2000 people form the nucleus of this city, called Auroville.

The report explained: "The project embodies the ideal of self-education, and sixteen nationalities are represented in the community. Simple labour-oriented industries, such as a press, a hand-made paper factory, a polyester unit, a mechanical workshop, pre-cast concrete works and various handicraft centres have been started . . . A small weatherstation has been established, and experiments are being carried out using wind energy to generate power. Four windmills are now in operation for pumping water from depths of 80 feet. Several solar-powered units have also been introduced."

The community is experimenting with biological agriculture, plans to develop deep sea fisheries and operates a 24-hour free medical service.

Commonwealth co-operation in the press and broadcasting has existed for many years. The Commonwealth Press Union was founded as long ago as 1909 (when it was the Empire Press Union). It has several hundred members representing the broad interests of those who run the leading newspapers, periodicals and news agencies in the Commonwealth. It holds conferences in various parts of the Commonwealth and organises fellowships, scholarships and other schemes to help journalists. Recently it has become particularly concerned with press freedom, which in an increasing number of Commonwealth countries is becoming a thing of the past.

Although depressing, this is hardly surprising, since the Western concept of press freedom has been subjected to fierce critical analysis by Third World governments. One favourite proposition is that a press which regards itself as in a sense the adversary of the government may be appropriate in a developed country but is unsuitable for a newly-independent country, where the first imperative is the forging of national unity. This is an attractive argument to those in authority, but it has clear dangers. Carried to its logical conclusion, it means accepting a government monopoly on the dissemination of information —

how else can "destructive" criticism be stifled? But if there is no legitimate means of expressing dissent, then illegitimate means will be found — coups, assassinations, terrorism. This indeed is the situation of many countries in Latin America, Asia and Africa — as the political prisoners in their gaols testify.

More recently a new argument has been heard — that information is dominated by the Western media — a form of imperialism — and that as a result events are reported through Western eyes. This gives a distorted picture of developments in the Third World, and, to make matters worse, Third World countries have to rely on these same Western media — mostly the major news agencies — for news about each other. To counteract this, news agencies in Third World countries are entering into pooling arrangements with each other, so that they no longer have to rely entirely on, for instance, Reuter (British) or the Associated Press (America).

The complaint of Third World countries has some force. The dominance of the Western media is a relic of imperial days, and Western journalists themselves often don't understand the Third World and interpret it through a cloud of preconceptions. The contempt in which the press is so often held is largely due to its own faults.

But, this having been said, there are some points to make on the other side. One is that a pooling of government-controlled news agencies is going to be heavily biased in favour of the official line in all countries, which is not always the same thing as the truth, to put it no more forcibly. We should not, after all, fall into the error of supposing that the interests of governments are always necessarily those of their people.

Two examples illustrate this. One is the famine in Ethiopia in 1973, which was brought to the attention of the world by the wicked Western media (in this case primarily television) when the government itself was concealing the news, preferring to let its people starve than admit it couldn't cope. The other was Bangladesh. I was there during the disastrous cyclone of 1970 (when it was still East Pakistan), and I was thanked by a Bengali official, not for anything I had done personally but as a representative of the Western press, which had reported the gravity of the situation and the inefficiency of the government in dealing with it. Some months later the Pakistan government removed the representatives of the Western press from Dacca before beginning its military action against the Bengalis. Two Western journalists, however, managed to remain by going into hiding, and they reported the truth of that merciless military crackdown. It was not until a good deal later that the people of Pakistan itself learned that their government had lied to them consistently during this period.

This is a complex subject, and there is no room to discuss it fully in these pages. It is, unfortunately, a new source of conflict between the developed and developing world, and, as in all conflicts, the first casualty will be the truth.

The Commonwealth Broadcasting Association was founded in 1945 as a result of wartime collaboration. It links national broadcasting organisations in more than 40 Commonwealth countries and dependencies, a condition being that they must have a commitment to public service broadcasting. This is a somewhat elusive concept, but essentially it means that, even if revenue is derived from advertising, public service broadcasting must serve the public good and not be subservient to commercial interests. It can be, of course, and frequently is, subservient to government interests.

The activities of the CBA are extensive. According to its official handbook: "There cannot be a single day in any year on which professional broadcasters across the Commonwealth are not engaged in some act of collaboration with colleagues elsewhere, whether it be in arranging an exchange of programme material, in organising special coverage of a Commonwealth event, in studying abroad some facet of broadcasting practice or participating at home or overseas in a training project or merely in writing an informal letter to a colleague abroad to sustain a personal link established by a previous encounter."

More formally there is a considerable degree of training. This began as long ago as 1933 when the BBC sent expert staff to India and Canada to help set up broadcasting services. After the war demand increased enormously, and all over the Commonwealth there are now radio and television services modelled on those of the BBC, with all its faults and virtues.

However, like the rest of the Commonwealth, the CBA is becoming increasingly less dependent on Britain, and a number of other countries now provide training facilities. The Association holds regular conferences in different parts of the Commonwealth. Since 1968 there has been a "Commonwealth pool" for coverage of the Olympic Games. Sport, in fact, is an area in which Commonwealth broadcasting organisation are frequently collaborating, covering athletics, cricket and rugby, for example.

Two comparatively small Commonwealth organisations which stress the value of personal links deserve a mention. They are the Women's Corona Society and the Victoria League.

The first is open to women of all nationalities and has branches in more than 30 countries. Its aim is to "promote friendship and understanding", and among the services it provides are briefing courses for British women going overseas and programmes for women from other countries going to Britain. It has a panel of speakers who give talks on Commonwealth countries and holds regular conferences on subjects of interest to women. The topic chosen for 1977 was "The World's Food — What's for To-morrow?"

The Victoria League for Commonwealth Friendship dates from 1901. It welcomes visitors to Britain from other parts of the Commonwealth, provides them with a chance to meet English people and runs two hostels for students — in London and Birmingham. The League has branches in several other Commonwealth countries, notably Canada, where it is called the Imperial Order of Daughters of the Empire. Its definition of the Commonwealth is a little eccentric, comprising those countries which were members in 1921. Thus it still has branches in South Africa, which left the Commonwealth in 1961.

In 1975 it moved its headquarters to the Royal Commonwealth Society building in London — an appropriate choice, since the Society is the senior of all the voluntary Commonwealth bodies. It was founded in 1868 under the name of the Colonial Society.

Like the Commonwealth itself, the RCS has had to adapt to a changed role over the years, and some members have done so more successfully than others. Until the end of the 1950s very few Africans frequented its premises[2] and, although it has branches in many countries, its membership is dominated by the white Commonwealth. It has been the work of a few dedicated people which has enabled it to

(2) The History of the Royal Commonwealth Society by Trevor R. Reese (OUP, 1968).

remain forward-looking and not to indulge in a sort of imperial nostalgia. As its own Secretary-General has put it, the thinking of some of the branches "has been so out of touch with the modern Commonwealth as to be counter-productive".

The Society has several quite distinct activities. It was founded in part to provide a meeting place in London for visitors from the colonies, and this, given the change in their status, it still does. It has an active social side, and its headquarters near Trafalgar Square provide the facilities of a residential club, with bedrooms, bars and a restaurant. The building also contains one of the finest Commonwealth libraries in the world and facilities for conferences. Lectures and discussions take place there regularly, and many distinguished Commonwealth statesmen have addressed the Society.

It publishes every two months a journal called "Commonwealth", available to the general public and dealing in a lively manner with topics of Commonwealth and general international interest (and to which I have the honour to contribute a regular column). It runs the study group tours and the essay competition for school children mentioned in Chapter Five. It is also in practice a spokesman for all the voluntary organisations in the Commonwealth and seeks to enlarge their influence.

In a leaflet published in 1974 the Royal Commonwealth Society explained its policy of seeking support for the unofficial Commonwealth — what are called in the language of international bureaucracy non-governmental organisations (or, even worse, NGOs). Its aim, it said, was to promote throughout the world an understanding of the nature and working of the Commonwealth.

"Underlying this aim is the belief that the Commonwealth is an important influence for good in the world. It has grown into a community committed to work together for the improvement of the quality of life. It is based on the principle of the equality and freedom of all individuals, regardless of differences of race, culture or creed."

The Society proposed the formation of an organisation or grouping of organisations in each of the member countries. It would be created by local initiative, and the object would be "to draw together from a wide variety of backgrounds and specialised interests all those who share a belief in the Commonwealth as an instrument of international co-operation".

In 1976 the RCS submitted a paper to a meeting of senior officials of Commonwealth governments in Canberra, Australia, a meeting which is held regularly now in the years between the heads of government conferences. The paper argued that the voluntary organisations in the Commonwealth had a great deal to offer, since they provided a considerable reservoir of knowledge, experience and enthusiasm. But their capacity to contribute was un-coordinated and under-utilised. It suggested that Commonwealth governments and the Secretariat might help these organisations to identify their roles and work out plans of action.

Later in 1976 a conference was held at Dalhousie University, Nova Scotia, to discuss that very subject. Representatives of a number of voluntary organisations met to consider their contributions to the development of the Commonwealth and their relationship to the official, governmental Commonwealth. It recommended, among other things, that the scope of the Commonwealth Foundation should be broadened — and its income increased — so that it could help not only professional associations but all voluntary organisations with a contribution to make to Commonwealth objectives.

Clearly there is a good way to go still in making full use of the potential offered by all these organisations. They have grown up haphazardly over the years, fulfilling special needs, and it is only recently that the idea of co-operation among themselves has really caught on. There are clear dangers, too, in linking them too closely with the governmental machinery.

However, all these qualifications having been made, the development of the unofficial Commonwealth is one of the most interesting and exciting possibilities for the future. The examples given in this chapter, and elsewhere in the book, show something of the variety and range of the organisations which comprise it. Their great virtue is that they are voluntary, not aspects of government. They are the basic Commonwealth, the Commonwealth of people who have found a purpose and seek to serve it.

CHAPTER ELEVEN

Commonwealth Culture

One day in March 1975 a group of sixty people from 15 Commonwealth countries began an experiment in Malta which a professor of music described as "a nonsense". To celebrate the opening of a new cultural centre just outside Valetta they held a "Commonwealth Folk" seminar of music and dancing.

The *Times of Malta* reported: "Within a week of their meeting for the first time musicians, dancers and singers were working together in the international groups to perfect items in African, Asian, Caribbean and European idioms. An Indian folk dance was performed convincingly by a team including only one Indian together with a Maltese, a Fijian and a Hong Kong Chinese; musicians from Britain, Ghana, Kenya, Malta, Nigeria, Sierra Leone and Uganda achieved complete understanding in the interpretation of African rhythms; singers from eight countries in all parts of the world harmonised in traditional songs from the Caribbean."

Performances were given in theatres and, informally, in the streets. If it was nonsense, commented the director, then it was delightful nonsense; it succeeded beyond all expectations.

Those taking part had some minor reservations. One thought there were too many elements to be fitted into too short a time but added: "We proved that it is possible to put together persons from vastly different races and backgrounds and that, given a project dear to their hearts, they will get to know each other quickly and work together with an amazing degree of harmony, and this in itself breaks down barriers and promotes understanding."

Others thought it proved the value of the Commonwealth and suggested that it should be followed up in some way. And, in fact, the

Malta experiment did lead to the setting up of a Commonwealth Arts Association later the same year. Its objects were described as being to encourage the development of the arts in Commonwealth countries and their appreciation throughout the Commonwealth; to provide links between existing arts associations and between artists and the organisations and institutions with which they work; and to promote performances, exhibitions, workshops and seminars embracing the cultures and arts forms of the Commonwealth.

The "Commonwealth Folk" project was sponsored by the government of Malta and the Commonwealth Secretariat in association with the Commonwealth Institute, another long-established body whose role has changed considerably over the years. It was founded as the Imperial Institute in 1893, and its objects were: "To promote the utilisation of the commercial and industrial resources of the Empire by the chemical and technical investigation of raw materials and the supply of information relating to such materials and their production; to maintain a comprehensive exhibition illustrating the life, scenery and progress of all the countries of the Empire; and to organise other services designed to spread a knowledge of the life and work of its peoples." It still fulfils the last two of these three aims, but not quite in the way envisaged.

It is now a grant-aided organisation with an independent board of governors, including the High Commissioners in London of all the Commonwealth countries. It describes itself as a centre for information about the Commonwealth, "a supermarket of resources and activities." It is housed in a splendid modern building in Kensington, London, which was opened in 1962.

In this building there are permanent exhibitions of all the Commonwealth countries, paid for by each government. These use a variety of imaginative display techniques and are visited and admired by thousands of people who come as individuals or in school groups. In 1975 the total attendance was over half a million. There is also a combined theatre and cinema, an art gallery, a library, which contains books, periodicals and audio-visual materials, and a shop selling books, crafts, posters and souvenirs from many countries. The arts of the Commonwealth are frequently on display, for example in the form of African drumming or West Indian story telling.

The Institute also organises conferences for schools and colleges of education and courses for senior pupils and teachers. It has produced a Commonwealth Study Kit and fact sheets about individual countries. To take its message outside London it has devised a travelling exhibition called the Commonwealth Caravan, which enlists the help of local people, including ethnic minorities, wherever it goes.

The Commonwealth Institute also exists in Scotland, with premises in Edinburgh, but not at present in any other Commonwealth country. This is a pity, because the British are not the only people who need to be educated about the modern Commonwealth. It is largely a question of finance, of course. Exhibitions are expensive, and many Commonwealth governments are poor and with plenty of calls on their resources. But perhaps a start could be made with regional institutes, to which several governments could jointly contribute. After all, in so far as the Commonwealth has a cultural centre, it is the Institute.

The countries of the Commonwealth have a wide variety of cultures, using the word in the narrow sense of art-forms. There is the musical scene in the Caribbean, for example, there are music and dancing from India and the surrounding countries, folksong from a score of traditions, African sculpture. The experiment in Malta featured some of them, but every country has its own contribution to make. As the report on the Malta festival put it: "Cultural factors in recent years have been largely subordinated to economic considerations in the minds of most policy makers and administrators. This Commonwealth function served to mark a growing realisation that culture is inextricably bound up with the development process and that cultural differences can bring people together in mutual tolerance and appreciation instead of dividing them, as has happened so frequently in the past."

The unity in diversity which is a feature of the Commonwealth is shown, too, in literature. The study of Commonwealth literature is of comparatively recent origin; it dates from the 1960s. The term is used to cover literature written in English outside Britain and the United States and therefore includes an enormous range of writers — for example, V.S. Naipaul, Patrick White, Doris Lessing, Wilson Harris, Mordecai Richler, Wole Soyinka.

These writers — and many more names could be added to the list

— represent very different types of experience, but they have in common the English language and in addition the impact on their societies which comes from association with Britain, however remote. The impact, of course, is different in each case. I remember an African newspaper editor, educated at Oxford, who was passionately fond of English poetry and quoted chunks of Shakespeare at me. But, he said, his children would learn about African culture and not simply become replicas of educated Britons. The literature produced by tensions of this sort will be very unlike that produced by, say, an Australian, who can take the British cultural heritage more easily for granted.

Leeds University in Britain organised the first conference on Commonwealth literature in 1964. In an opening address Professor Norman Jeffares explained[1]: "What is needed is an awareness of how the traditions of English literature have been continued, adapted or rejected in the different countries of the Commonwealth. In other words, the Australian critic, and through him the Australian reading public — and the Australian writer — would benefit from a knowledge of how similar scenes are treated by Canadian writers. The Nigerian schoolchild or student who anxiously asks a visitor what the visitor thinks of Nigerian writing in English would be the better able to answer his own query if he had read Narayan's novels about that imaginary Indian town Malgudi and had thus begun to work out his own comparative judgements, to expand his intellectual horizons. In the same way we have found here in Leeds that our inevitable insular English graduates are delighted by the discovery of expanding horizons when they read Commonwealth literature."

As a result of the Leeds conference, an Association for Commonwealth Literature and Language Studies was set up. This has operated in an interesting way in three-year cycles. In each cycle the officers and secretariat have been in one country; at the end of the three years they have organised a conference, then new officers have taken over in a different country. The association began in Britain and has since been administered from Canada, Uganda and India. A European branch was formed in 1972, with Anna Rutherford, an Australian who has actively promoted the study of Commonwealth literature in the Uni-

(1) Commonwealth Literature (Heinemann, 1965).

versity of Aarhus in Denmark, as chairman. A Canadian association was formed in 1973. ACLAS publishes a newsletter, and there is in addition the Journal of Commonwealth Literature, which began publication after the Leeds conference.

However, not all the recommendations of the conference resulted in practical action. For one thing, it argued that, if a Commonwealth Secretariat were to be set up, it should have a strong cultural division. The Secretariat was set up the following year but has no cultural division at all, not even a weak one.

One reason for this is presumably that those involved in the Secretariat have been politicians, who have decided on the tasks it should undertake, and civil servants, who have executed those tasks — not a poet among them. The Western attitude to cultural activities — something you do, or watch others doing, in any time you have to spare from earning a living — is still dominant. But perhaps the more deeply-rooted attitude is becoming better understood. In less highly specialised societies than those of the West, culture — music, dancing, sculpture, poetry, for instance — is an integral part of life, not an optional extra; this is what the West has lost.

This is not a particularly new or original thought, but it needs to be re-stated. It was well put 30 years ago by the American poet Oscar Williams, and, although he was referring in particular to poetry, his remarks can be taken as applying to all the arts: "This art is neither an extraneous growth upon the pragmatic activity which has become so universally synonymous with existence, nor an obsolete organ like the appendix. On the contrary, it is the ichor which man's spiritual nature secretes for the purpose of healing the kind of wounds from which we today suffer. Just as medical science used to make the mistake of draining off the very blood needed to restore health, modern society is ever busy trying to dry up the real essence of the arts, because their usefulness has been forgotten and not re-discovered."

Perhaps the Commonwealth can help in the re-discovery.

any public notice at all because it had one devoted press officer (happily, still there). The Information Division was set up in 1971 and the staff increased, but it is still less than a dozen, including secretaries. It produces press releases, pamphlets, feature articles and a diary of events. Its staff brief journalists, help to draft speeches and answer queries and keep in touch with member governments on the flow of information. A recent innovation is the production of radio programmes on tape.

The division's expenditure for the year 1975/76 was just over £71 000 — barely enough to buy a year's supply of tea and biscuits for the information officers employed by the member governments. To make a simple comparison, in the same period more than £300 000 was spent on advertising a single brand of shampoo in Britain alone. And one of the country's biggest advertisers, Kelloggs, are estimated to spend three and a half million pounds a year in publicising their products.

I am not suggesting that the Commonwealth should be marketed like a breakfast cereal, but the present amount devoted to information seems to rest on the assumption either that an informed public opinion is unnecessary or that the virtues of the Commonwealth are self-evident. Alas, they are not. There is, as we have seen, considerable misunderstanding about the nature of the association, and, partly as a result, there are criticisms.

One particular line of criticism is founded, in Britain, on the fact that the Commonwealth is no longer the Empire and, in other countries, on the belief that it still is. It is frequently held that the association was dreamed up so that Britain could retain her influence even after giving her colonies independence. British governments have sometimes acted as if they, too, believed this, but, if it ever was true, it is not to-day. This hasn't prevented people in some Third World countries from demanding withdrawal from the Commonwealth whenever they are in dispute with Britain. It happened in India during the Suez crisis of 1956, in Africa during the controversy over British arms sales to South Africa in 1970, and it recurred in Nigeria as late as 1976, when Anglo-Nigerian relations went through a strained period.

During his period as Secretary-General Mr. Arnold Smith spent a good deal of time arguing with Commonwealth leaders that, even if they didn't agree with the British, leaving the Commonwealth was not the way to express their disagreement; the Commonwealth, after all, is a great deal more than Britain. He seems to have succeeded with most governments — Pakistan is an obvious exception — but the message hasn't got through to all their people.

In Britain the average attitude to the Commonwealth is probably one of indifference based on misunderstanding, but there is a fair degree of hostility on the right. For example: "An institution so uniquely and sublimely preposterous can surely never die. The British Commonwealth is the degenerate heir of the British Empire, an heir whose least affliction is a kind of political delirium tremens."[1]

This is the voice of the romantic right, of those who argue that it is one thing to rule over all those funny coloured chaps but quite another to be expected to treat them as equals. It is similar to the voice which campaigns against Commonwealth immigrants, while accepting the results of their labours.

However, the fact that some criticisms of the Commonwealth are clearly based on ignorance of its actual functions doesn't mean that it is therefore beyond criticism. There is one very obvious question to be asked and that is: Is it necessary? It does, after all, take up time and money, it employs expertise which might perhaps be put to better use, it is a great begetter of windy rhetoric. Is its continued existence justified?

One of the great growth areas in the past 30 years has been the international bureaucracy. Politicians, civil servants, academics, advisers, consultants and experts of all sorts (and journalists) jet around the world at enormous public expense attending conferences, seminars, workshops and indulging in "valuable exchanges of experience" and "meaningful dialogues". Some have privileges denied to ordinary mortals, such as tax-free salaries and other goodies; they are virtually a new privileged class. Many of their activities have been outlined in previous chapters, and it would be obscurantist to argue that they have achieved nothing. Clearly in an increasingly interdependent world it is vital that contacts should continue at as many different levels as possible.

But it is legitimate to ask whether the results have been commen-

(1) "Peter Simple", *The Daily Telegraph,* July 1976.

surate with the manhours taken up. This is not a frivolous point. After all, the Food and Agriculture Organisation of the United Nations had to be drastically pruned because practically its entire budget was going towards paying for its staff, with little over for actual projects. The fact that it reached this point is an indication of the tendency of bureaucracy to proliferate, almost irrespective of the functions it performs.

The Commonwealth, of course, is a minnow in this pond, with an annual budget and staff for its Secretariat a mere fraction of any of the main United Nations agencies. Nevertheless, in percentage terms it has grown considerably; already Marlborough House has become too small for it, and some of its staff are housed in other buildings. So far the growth has been commensurate with its increased functions, and there is a conscious aim of ensuring that it gives value for money. Long may this continue — but it will need to be watched.

And, of course, even if it were shown that the Commonwealth is being run as efficiently and cheaply as possible, it would still be legitimate to ask whether it were performing a function which could be better performed by any of the other multilateral agencies which abound on the world scene. What's so special about the Commonwealth?

One of the troubles is that in the past it was oversold. It was seen by some enthusiasts as a "Third Force" between the superpowers or as an example of how people of many different races could show the world how to co-operate. This example is still valid up to a point, but bitter arguments over a fundamentally racial issue — white minority regimes in southern Africa — caused the association to slump in public esteem. Now, as a consequence, it is under-valued.

The theme of this book has been that there is something special about it, and the evidence supports this view. This is not a question of personal preference on my part. I was originally as sceptical as the best of right-wing journalists and regarded the whole institution as the result of a historical accident, destined eventually to wither away. But the testimony of those working in the Commonwealth and my own experience in covering its activities have forced me to the conviction that it has a unique atmosphere and a unique role.

There is no point in making exaggerated claims for it. It will never be a major world political force; it couldn't even prevent two of its own members, Indian and Pakistan, from fighting each other. But it has a lot to give in a more modest way. The message that keeps recurring is that it is easier to get things done through the Commonwealth than through any other multilateral institution. It is partly a question of language, partly of similarity of outlook. The combination gives immediate gains in informality and flexibility, the two words which are used so often to sum up the advantages of the Commonwealth that they have become platitudes. But the point about platitudes, of course, is that they are true. We may consider ourselves fortunate to have such an association to hand, even if it is a historical accident. This is particularly so now that its role is being seen as not simply to serve its own members but to act as a kind of laboratory or test bed for the whole international community — what the Secretary-General has called a sample of humanity at the service of humanity.

But, of course, an important question remains. It is easy enough to see the advantages of membership for the developing countries, especially the smaller ones. But if the Commonwealth is simply another tool for helping the Third World, what do its richer members get out of it? In particular, what does Britain get out of it, now that it's no longer the leader? There are several possible answers, but none are simple or straightforward.

One was suggested by what I was told of the official British attitude to the Commonwealth Youth Programme. In essence, this was to see it as an aid project, worth supporting with money but not apparently as something from which young British people might benefit. This is symptomatic of the official British attitude to the Commonwealth as a whole and may be part of the explanation for the indifference with which it is regarded by the public. At the bottom of this attitude is really a profound arrogance, an assumption that Britain is the one which has things to give while the others more or less gratefully receive. It is an assumption of complete superiority in all things, an assumption which can be seen to be absurd when it is actually put into words but is, I think, unconsciously held by many English people. Perhaps it is only those who remember the British Empire who feel this way; in which case there is a hope that British people will come to accept the benefits other Commonwealth countries can bestow on them, in insights and enrichment of their lives.

Another argument, which has been put by the Secretary-General, rests on the fact that Britain is a large importer of raw materials. The producers of many of them are in the Third World and increasingly are uniting to secure better terms. Being in the Commonwealth opens a door to them, and in the years ahead this will be seen more and more to be of advantage to Britain.

The distinguished academic and diplomat, Dr. Davidson Nicol of Sierra Leone, has suggested that, with the increasing power of the Afro-Asian nations, the Commonwealth is becoming more valuable to Britain than the other way round. In the Commonwealth lecture at Cambridge University in February 1975 he had this to say: "The presence of Britain as a permanent member of the Security Council should logically be linked with the Commonwealth, because when it was given that privileged position it was a major partner in a victorious team and a major force in world strategy. The war is over, and with the voluntary relinquishing of the Empire the world-wide network of British strategic power has been diminished. But, as the representative of the group of more than 30 nations constituting about a third of the world's population, Britain's position as a permanent member of the Security Council is justifiable. Without this connection it would be difficult to see why, if the United Nations is to be restructured, other nations should not have equal power with Britain. It would be an easy trap set by her enemies for Britain to fall into if it underestimates the power and the usefulness of the Commonwealth."

These are all rather sophisticated arguments, however true. They are not the sort to kindle enthusiasm for the association, and this perhaps is the key to the whole problem of public indifference. In 1973 there was a debate in the House of Lords in London on Commonwealth consultation, a rare event which has not, so far as I know, been repeated. A certain amount of nonsense was talked, but some constructive suggestions were put forward. For instance, a bishop argued that the shared military traditions of the Commonwealth made it suitable as the nucleus of an international police force — a contribution from the Church Militant which doesn't seem to have been followed up.

Complaints were made that not enough was known about the modern Commonwealth, and in particular that it was largely ignored in schools. And Baroness White, after referring to "the really fantastic amount of co-operation" that goes on between Commonwealth countries continued: "We do not dramatise this sufficiently for the general public; the general public is hardly aware of what is going on. The people who are themselves engaged in certain professions know more or less what goes on in their own profession. But there is nothing to catch the imagination, nothing to touch the heart about all this."

Precisely.

After this debate I wrote[2]: "The Commonwealth comprises a quarter of mankind. Yet how many of these millions are aware of it as a factor in their lives? And of those few who are aware of it, how many regard it simply as a bilateral relationship — between Britain and their country — instead of the multilateral relationship it has become?

"Where is the Commonwealth association of bank clerks? Or railwaymen? Or dock workers? Where is the link between the broad mass of people living in the five continents of the world? Where, for that matter, are the individuals who have benefited from the immense amount of intra-Commonwealth work that goes on? We should be hearing their stories.

"That is a large number of questions, and no answers are offered, at the back of the book or anywhere else. There are many far better qualified than I to suggest the answers . . . But the questions really boil down to one: is there the political will among the Commonwealth leaders to try to capture the imagination of their people with a vision of what this unique association might become?"

The answer, so far, is clearly "No", but it is perhaps worth repeating the question.

(2) "Commonwealth", August 1973.

Members of the Commonwealth
(as at October 1976)

Note: Countries described as monarchies recognise the Queen as their head of state. All countries recognise the Queen as Head of the Commonwealth.

AUSTRALIA
Population:	13 338 300
Area:	7 720 887 sq. km.
Independence:	Commonwealth of Australia created by proclamation, 1901.
Status:	Monarchy.

BAHAMAS
Population:	200 000
Area:	13 995 sq. km.
Independence:	1973
Status:	Monarchy.

BANGLADESH
Population:	71 479 071
Area:	143 407 sq. km.
Independence:	Became a separate state 1971 (formerly part of Pakistan)
Status:	Republic.

BARBADOS
Population:	247 500
Area:	431 sq. km.
Independence:	1966
Status:	Monarchy.

BOTSWANA

Population:	675 000
Area:	572 000 sq. km. (estimated)
Independence:	1966
Status:	Republic.

BRITAIN

Population:	55 968 300
Area:	242 005 sq. km.
Status:	Monarchy.

CANADA

Population:	22 446 300
Area:	10 020 314 sq. km.
Independence:	Dominion of Canada created by British North America Act, 1867
Status:	Monarchy.

CYPRUS

Population:	660 000
Area:	9 292 sq. km.
Independence:	1960
Status:	Republic.

FIJI

Population:	559 813
Area:	18 353 sq. km.
Independence:	1970
Status:	Monarchy.

THE GAMBIA

Population:	495 000
Area:	10 413 sq. km.
Independence:	1965
Status:	Republic (1970).

GHANA

Population:	9 200 000
Area:	238 925 sq. km.
Independence:	1957
Status:	Republic (1960).

GRENADA
Population:	110 000
Area:	312 sq. km.
Independence:	1974
Status:	Monarchy.

GUYANA
Population:	830 000
Area:	215 920 sq. km.
Independence:	1966
Status:	Co-operative Republic (1970).

INDIA
Population:	604 000 000
Area:	3 282 560 sq. km.
Independence:	1947
Status:	Republic.

JAMAICA
Population:	1 982 700
Area:	11 446 sq. km.
Independence:	1962
Status:	Monarchy.

KENYA
Population:	12 000 000
Area:	585 223 sq. km.
Independence:	1963
Status:	Republic (1964).

LESOTHO
Population:	1 181 330
Area:	30 478 sq. km.
Independence:	1966
Status:	Own monarchy.

MALAWI
Population:	4 916 000
Area:	118 134 sq. km.
Independence:	1964
Status:	Republic (1966).

MALAYSIA

Population:	11 930 000
Area:	333 787 sq. km.
Independence:	Federation of Malaya 1957
	Federation of Malaysia 1963
Status:	Own monarchy.

MALTA

Population:	419 000
Area:	317 sq. km.
Independence:	1964
Status:	Republic (1974).

MAURITIUS

Population:	881 944
Area:	1977 sq. km.
Independence:	1968
Status:	Monarchy.

NAURU

Population:	7000
Area:	21 sq. km.
Independence:	1968
Status:	Republic.

Note: Nauru is a special member. It does not attend heads of government meetings but otherwise has all the normal rights of membership.

NEW ZEALAND

Population:	3 100 000
Area:	269 864 sq. km.
Independence:	1907 (Dominion created)
Status:	Monarchy.

NIGERIA

Population:	79 759 000
Area:	927 859 sq. km.
Independence:	1960
Status:	Republic (1963)

PAPUA NEW GUINEA

Population:	2 570 780
Area:	463 735 sq. km.
Independence:	1975
Status:	Monarchy.

SEYCHELLES

Population:	60 000
Area:	310 sq. km.
Independence:	1976
Status:	Republic.

SIERRA LEONE

Population:	3 000 000
Area:	72 645 sq. km.
Independence:	1961
Status:	Republic (1971).

SINGAPORE

Population:	2 219 100
Area:	587 sq. km.
Independence:	1965
Status:	Republic.

SRI LANKA

Population:	13 180 000
Area:	65 900 sq. km.
Independence:	1948
Status:	Republic (1972).

SWAZILAND

Population:	494 396
Area:	17 400 sq. km.
Independence:	1968
Status:	Own monarchy

TANZANIA

Population:	14 500 000
Area:	946 170 sq. km.
Independence:	Tanganyika 1961
	Zanzibar 1963
	Union 1964
Status:	Republic.

TONGA
Population:	90 000
Area:	702 sq. km.
Independence:	1970
Status:	Own monarchy.

TRINIDAD AND TOBAGO
Population:	1 033 000
Area:	5 020 sq. km.
Independence:	1962
Status:	Republic (1976).

UGANDA
Population:	10 500 000
Area:	236 930 sq. km.
Independence:	1962
Status:	Republic (1967).

WESTERN SAMOA
Population:	151 251
Area:	2853 sq. km.
Independence:	1962
Status:	Own monarchy.

ZAMBIA
Population:	4 500 000
Area:	755 983 sq. km.
Independence:	1964
Status:	Republic.

(Details supplied by the Commonwealth Institute).

In addition to these independent states there are a number of dependencies, mostly British, and including such territories as Hong Kong, Belize and Gibraltar; some are being prepared for independence. There are also five Associated States among the small islands of the Eastern Caribbean. The British government remains responsible for their defence and external affairs, but they are internally self-governing and have announced their desire for full independence eventually.

The Commonwealth Declaration of Principles

Commonwealth Heads of government unanimously approved the following Declaration of Principles at their meeting in Singapore in January 1971:

The Commonwealth of Nations is a voluntary association of independent sovereign states, each responsible for its own policies, consulting and co-operating in the common interests of their people and in the promotion of international understanding and world peace.

Members of the Commonwealth come from territories in the six continents and five oceans, include people of different races, languages and religions, and display every stage of economic development from poor developing nations to wealthy industrialised nations. They encompass a rich variety of cultures, traditions and institutions.

Membership of the Commonwealth is compatible with the freedom of member governments to be non-aligned or to belong to any other grouping, association or alliance. Within this diversity all members of the Commonwealth hold certain principles in common. It is by pursuing these principles that the Commonwealth can continue to influence international society for the benefit of mankind.

We believe that international peace and order are essential to the security and prosperity of mankind; we therefore support the United Nations and seek to strengthen its influence for peace in the world and its efforts to remove the causes of tension between nations.

We believe in the liberty of the individual, in equal rights for all citizens regardless of race, colour, creed or political belief, and in their inalienable right to participate by means of free and democratic political processes in framing the society in which they live. We therefore strive to promote in each of our countries those representative institutions and guarantees for personal freedom under the law that are our common heritage.

We recognise racial prejudice as a dangerous sickness threatening the healthy development of the human race and racial discrimination as an unmitigated evil of society. Each of us will vigorously combat this evil within our own nation. No country will afford to regimes which practise racial discrimination assistance which in its own judgement directly contributes to the pursuit or consolidation of this evil policy. We oppose all forms of colonial domination and racial oppression and are committed to the principles of human dignity and equality.

We will therefore use all our efforts to foster human equality and dignity everywhere and to further the principles of self-determination and non-racialism.

We believe that the wide disparities in wealth now existing between different sections of mankind are too great to be tolerated. They also create world tensions. Our aim is their progressive removal. We therefore seek to use our efforts to overcome poverty, ignorance and disease, in raising standards of life and achieving a more equitable international society. To this end our aim is to achieve the freest possible flow of international trade on terms fair and equitable to all, taking into account the special requirements of the developing countries, and to encourage the flow of adequate resources, including governmental and private resources, to the developing countries, bearing in mind the importance of doing this in a true spirit of partnership and of establishing for this purpose in the developing countries conditions which are conducive to sustained investment and growth.

We believe that international co-operation is essential to remove the cause of war, promote tolerance, combat injustice and secure development among the peoples of the world. We are convinced that the Commonwealth is one of the most fruitful associations for these purposes.

In pursuing these principles the members of the Commonwealth believe that they can provide a constructive example of the multi-national approach which is vital to peace and progress in the modern world. The association is based on consultation, discussion and co-operation.

In rejecting coercion as an instrument of policy they recognise that the security of each member state from external aggression is a matter for concern to all members. It provides many channels for continuing exchanges of knowledge and views on professional, cultural, economic, legal and political issues among member states.

These relationships we intend to foster and extend, for we believe that our multi-national association can expand human understanding and understanding among nations, assist in the elimination of discrimination based on differences of race, colour or creed, maintain and strengthen personal liberty, contribute to the enrichment of life for all and provide a powerful influence for peace among nations.

APPENDIX THREE

Sources of Information

"A Year Book of the Commonwealth" continues to be published by the British government and is obtainable through HM Stationery Office. It is an invaluable reference work, giving details of all Commonwealth countries, including dependencies, but excluding Britain itself. It also lists a large number of organisations in Britain with Commonwealth links.

The Commonwealth Secretariat, Marlborough House, Pall Mall, London SW1Y 5HX (01-839 3411), publishes reports of the Secretary-General, annual reports on Commonwealth trade and aid and reports of conferences and seminars. It also publishes a booklet "The Commonwealth Today" and pamphlets on the work of such bodies as the Commonwealth Fund for Technical Co-operation, the Commonwealth Foundation and the Secretariat itself. These are free.

The Commonwealth Institute, Kensington High Street, London W8 6NQ (01-602 3252), publishes facts sheets about member countries, a Commonwealth study kit, teachers' guides, commodity leaflets and pamphlets on such topics as "What is the Commonwealth" and "The Commonwealth in Action" (which covers briefly many of the activities mentioned in the book). For those visiting or living in London it is well worth a visit.

The Commonwealth Development Corporation, 33 Hill Street, London W1A 3AZ (01-629 8484), publishes an annual report. It has also produced a wall chart for schools, with an accompanying booklet listing its work in individual countries.

Periodicals

Commonwealth (bi-monthly), published by the Royal Commonwealth Society, 18 Northumberland Avenue, London WC2N 5BJ
(01-930 6733) *The Round Table* (quarterly), also published from 18
Northumberland Avenue (01-930 9993).

INDEX

125